Be The Nerd That's Heard

David Duffett

GeekSpeak
Press

First published by GeekSpeak Press in 2025

Editors: Martha Gee, Charmaine Houser

Cover Design: Richard Johnson, TheGang.biz

ISBN: 978-1-0683848-4-4

Acknowledgements

I would like, first and foremost, to thank God for His goodness and grace to me.

I would also like to thank people that have helped me on my way in life in general, and some that have specifically helped in the production and publishing of this book. These include, but are not limited to:

Jan Howard
Ed Joinson
Mike Booth
Graham "Arnold" Dawson
Larry Kavanagh
Peter Thomson
Ian Cooper
Nigel Playford
Chris Gravett
Alan Pound
Rusty Cone
John Shapiro
Mark Spencer
Jared Smith
Bill Hall
Leslie Smith Conway
Danny Windham
Tom Ziglar
Michelle Prince
Charmaine Houser
Murray Cowell
Jon Billett
Martha Gee
Alan Stevens
Darius Schnaare
Richard Johnson

Dedication

To my Mum and Dad, my wife Anemilse and my children Luke, Charmaine and Holly. Thank you for your love and support.

In loving memory of my brother Mark, who was the first published author in my family.

Let him that is taught in the word communicate unto him that teaches in all good things.
Be not deceived; God is not mocked: for whatsoever a man sows, that shall he also reap.
Galatians 6:6-7

Table of Contents

Foreword
by Mark Spencer

I first met David when we were both speakers at a telecommunications event in Dallas TX, in the early days of Asterisk just beginning to make its way onto the world stage.

We were coming from nearly opposite ends of the telecommunications spectrum. He was working for an established company using very sophisticated equipment and I was working from a system which used stripped down minimal designs and highly leveraged the power of the computer upon which the system was running.

When it was David's turn to make his presentation, it was found that the 'clicker' supplied by the venue was not working, so I offered to be his clicker - by sitting at his laptop and advancing the slides when he nodded his head!

I recall him starting off with a fun exercise, asking the audience which shape they most associated with, the choices being a triangle, a square, a circle or a squiggly line. As an out of box thinker, I immediately knew I was the squiggly line! Based on each shape, David then provided a humorous description of each personality type, hitting mine directly on the head.

It was then I knew that David had special skills, not just for understanding and conveying technical topics himself, but for engaging with an audience to draw them into his presentation, and to deliver an understanding and an appreciation of the significance of those topics too.

Coming from the world of Open Source, I also knew that genuine engagement was even more critical than other environments because of the importance of the development and user communities. Unlike traditional development teams where they are being paid money for their time, the Asterisk development team consisted of thousands of programmers and users motivated not by traditional compensation, but by feelings.

If you wanted people to contribute, they needed to feel appreciated, heard, and that they were a part of the overall vision and direction of the project. This meant that communicating these things were imperative to the success of both Asterisk the project and Digium the company.

Because David's skills were so well aligned with the unique needs of community building, long before David worked at Digium, we encouraged him to be involved in AstriCon (our annual conference) where he brought attention to Asterisk for worldwide audiences and eventually went from providing attention grabbing presentations such as "Asterisk Mythbusters" and contests like "Fastest Dude to the Dialtone" (where community members raced against the clock to install and configure Asterisk to provide a working telephone line) to running the entire show as the Master of Ceremonies. As MC, David was able to help bridge audience participation and interest even between major presentations.

Eventually, we were fortunate enough to have David join Digium as the Worldwide Community Director for Asterisk Open Source, to best utilize his skills in the advancement of the project in the broadest possible way. While David did not direct our internal development team or run our sales or marketing process, in many ways he maximized the performance of both these areas within the company by effectively engaging and communicating with the Community at large.

During his time at Digium, David presented at many technical conferences all around the world, in addition to teaching Asterisk and delivering Presentation Skills training for our staff at Digium Headquarters in Huntsville, AL.

I'm delighted to see David expanding this influence and bringing his skills and experience to bear by empowering geeks like me to better express themselves. Now, he is not just providing benefits for Asterisk or Digium but for Engineers and technical professionals in general to help bridge the gap between finding a technical advantage, solution or approach and making it relevant to their chosen audiences.

In this book, David provides the easy-to-follow framework he has created to construct and deliver powerful presentations from scratch - or to optimise those you already have. This helps you to express the relevance and application of any technology you have, or to be an effective communicator for any other purpose.

Further, it also helps you better engage with your audience to make sure you properly ascertain what really matters to them, so that you can better adapt your approach (and technology, where appropriate) to fit their needs.

Mark Spencer
Creator of Asterisk and other Open Source projects
Founder of Avilution LLC and XFS Architect

Preface

The motivation to help Nerds be heard, to help technical people better communicate with others, and so have the value of their contributions more recognised, has its genesis many years ago as covered in chapter One.

The idea of writing a book to share ideas about exactly how to do that, in a specific way designed to resonate with technical people – so that they would find the information easy to receive, understand and implement came later.

This was largely due to the experience I gained while serving the Asterisk Community by speaking at many telecoms conferences (some specific to Asterisk, others more general) in various parts of the world.

As I sat and watched lots of other speakers deliver conference presentations and workshops, it cemented a feeling that had been growing within me over some years...

That the majority of people I watched and listened to at these conferences and events were very nice people. They were experts in their own fields of endeavour, they were people of whom it could be rightly said, **"They really know their stuff"**.

BUT, what I came to understand, as someone who was perhaps not as technical as some of these experts, is that **knowing your stuff is NOT enough!**

It is the ability to convey only the relevant parts of 'your stuff', at the correct technical level for your audience, in a way that really connects and resonates with them, that will truly get your message across in a memorable and engaging way.

I concluded that majority of people I saw had probably never been given any specific training on Communication or Presentation Skills, and they had probably picked up what they knew, or what they did by habit, from other people – who had never been appropriately trained either!

This, I believe, was because all their education and on-the-job learning had been focussed on the technical side of things, at the expense of developing their human-to-human interface and communication skills.

My mission, and the purpose of this book, is to help technical people develop their communications and presentation skills. And while the book is centred around making presentations – the content can equally usefully be applied to delivering demos and running meetings. The 7 Power Presenting Protocols could equally be called 7 Principles of Communication.

Now Nerds can be heard, Geeks can speak, Techies can talk, Engineers can engage their audiences and Propeller Heads can propel ahead! This book shows you how…

Chapter One - Who I Am, Why I Want to Help You, And How I Can Do It

Over many years of working in technical companies (mainly Telecoms), I have noticed that the technical people in these companies - who both created and supported the product or service - were not being recognised or rewarded anywhere near as well as the folk that went out and sold the product or service, and this seemed unfair to me.

It's not that I think the sales force should be rewarded less. Not at all. Sales itself is a very specialised area, and the most successful salesmen and women have their own set of highly effective skills and experience. To me, the issue was that the technical people were not getting the acknowledgment and rewards at the level I believe they deserve, and that is my reason for writing this book.

I believe that technical people (Nerds, Geeks) are undervalued, and I really, really want to help you - as a Geek – receive the rewards that are rightfully yours.

Thank you for investing in this book. I know that as you implement the proven 7 Power Presenting Protocols contained here you will reap the rewards of being a "Nerd that gets heard".

Why are Geeks so often not accorded the recognition they deserve? In my experience, it is not due to their supervisors or managers being unfair or unkind. Rather, it is that not enough people within companies truly understand the value of the specialised skills and experience that the technical people have, largely because the technical people themselves do not articulate that value at all, or at best do a bad job of it. In some cases, Geeks do not fully appreciate their own worth and the value of their contributions. If you do not realise your own value, you cannot communicate it to others. If you do understand your value but cannot effectively and persuasively communicate it to others, other people will not fully appreciate the value of what you are doing, and consequently, you are unlikely to receive the correct level of rewards for the role you fulfil. Obviously, the jobs market will help set pay levels for the various roles for a certain skillset combined with a demonstrable use of those skills, and a reliability in terms of showing up to do the job on a regular and consistent basis – but I am talking about a level of rewards beyond that.

There are many rewards for a "Nerd that gets heard"! Here are just a few examples:

Recognition

Having fellow team members, supervisors, managers, directors and the owners of a company (whether private individuals or shareholders) properly understand the value that you, as a Geek, of whatever technical persuasion, bring to the company can only be a good thing. This will lead to more recognition, ranging from a pat on the back or a "Thank you for a job well done!" to one or more of the following desirable outcomes...

Pay Rises

In addition to any annual salary increases that may occur as a matter of course during your employment in a given company (these are getting rarer as time goes by), there are other ways to gain an increase in your pay. There will usually be a bonus system or similar mechanism for upping someone's pay as recognition of merit or value added over time or during a particular project. There could also be recognition that your level of pay needs to be more competitive to match the level of what your given skillset is worth in the jobs market – but this is something that usually involves some persuasion on your part. Perhaps this is why salespeople are so successful at generating this type of reward – they are good at selling themselves! In both cases, the decision will be much easier to make when those with the power to give such increases truly understand the value that you bring to your work – and you can have a part to play in helping them come to that understanding.

Promotions

Imagine the difference between applying for an internal promotion, known as "one of the guys that sits over in the dark corner of the office where they write the code", compared with being properly recognised as "Simon – the guy that creates the software which analyses buying trends on our e-commerce system. Remember? He did that short lunchtime presentation a few weeks ago about the work of the team he's in". The difference is huge; Simon would be going in warm, and probably pushing against an open door, compared with the first guy – even though they might have very similar qualifications and technical skill levels.

New Job/New Company

Being able to represent yourself well in an interview situation is critical to your career progression. You would come across so much better if, when asked about your core technical skills, you could confidently assert that not only have you got them, but you have been able to share them in your current role – both by training others who need them, and by raising awareness of the need for them in a short presentation you did for the board, or at a local school etc! A good number of recruitment and selection processes now explicitly involve a presentation, but your ability to present yourself eloquently and with confidence is a key skill that those on the other side of the table will be looking for, even if a formal presentation is not initially required.

Raising Investment or Selling your Company

You're a Geek with a great idea. You've built up a business around that idea, and now you need funding, or you want to sell the company. A presentation is bound to be involved, and those you are presenting to, in a lot of cases, may not understand the technical details associated with what you are doing. Everything hangs on your ability to communicate your ideas, business plans and the reasons that your audience (large or small) should give you their money.

In short, as highlighted in each of the above cases, you only have value (in terms of what other people perceive) to the extent that you can personally communicate that value and/or have others testify to that value. Since it is infinitely more reliable to be able to do this yourself, rather than rely on a friend or colleague to do it for you, the smart Geek is the one that learns to speak for themselves!

The great news is that being able to speak in public is not some magic gift or black art. It is totally possible to learn this skill and, like many areas of life, there are just a few things that if done well, will absolutely transform the results you achieve through making you a better and more confident presenter.

I simply don't subscribe to the generalisation that Engineers (or other tech pros) are all introverts and cannot make great presenters and speakers.

My own belief is that while technical people were learning all the technical stuff during their education, and then in the world of work, it was often done at the expense of fully developing their communication skills.

Therefore, anyone with the right level of desire (and desire is the 'minimum system requirement' for this 'upgrade') can become a great communicator - and my mission is to accelerate that journey for you!

After many years of giving presentations and refining my approach, I have distilled the necessary skills and abilities into 7 Power Presenting Protocols that any Geek can adopt, adapt and become adept at. Sure, some people seem to have innate gifts that might help them to present well, but I firmly believe that anyone prepared to commit the time and effort can learn to implement these 7 Protocols and make exceptionally successful presentations - enabling them to reap the rewards of doing so in their career, and life in general!
However, before I get to identifying and explaining those Protocols, I would like to share the first part of my own story (find the full version at geekspeakhq.com), and why I've become so devoted to helping Geeks speak.

Background information, and what drives me to help

One of three boys, I was born in the small market town of Winslow, North Buckinghamshire in the United Kingdom and I was blessed to grow up in a loving Christian home.

Around the age of twelve, I saw my first CB (Citizen's Band) Radio, which had been brought into the UK from the USA. The thought of speaking to people remotely really appealed to me, and I began to soak up all the information I could about CB, saving up to get one of my own. So began a lifelong interest in communications, initially through radio and then through wired networks in the form of telephone systems.

My Dad worked as an Architectural Designer (he would later go on to qualify as a Chartered Architect) in the early Eighties and became interested in trying to harness the 'power' of some of the early personal computers in his line of work. This resulted in the acquisition of a Sinclair ZX81 Computer, followed by an early Apple II Europlus and then a BBC Microcomputer (an excellent and very versatile 6502-based machine) – all before the dawn of the ubiquitous x86-based PC.

Here, I found something else I was really interested in. Although I did some game-playing on some of these devices, I was much more interested in getting the computers to do something for me, by programming them – at that stage in the BASIC (Beginners All-purpose Symbolic Instruction Code) language. I began with just small things, like writing programs to create simple maths quizzes or to test myself with random questions when preparing for exams. Soon, I was trying to transmit computer programs stored as audio on cassette (yes, it was that long ago…) from one CB to another, and then to run the received programs on a remote computer.

Not knowing that one could go to college to learn about radio communications, I found my way on to a two-year Computer Studies course at a local college and learned programming in various languages of the day (ForTran, COBOL, BASIC, Pascal, etc.) along with computer hardware architecture. As this course was coming to an end, the teaching staff made me aware of a vacancy at the College to work in the Computer Studies Department (this was well before the term IT was in common use) and I was interested, so I applied. The interview with the College management (including the Vice Principal, a man called Ed Joinson – he will show up again later) went very well, so I was shocked when they awarded me a DIFFERENT job!

Apparently, they thought the interview went well too but concluded that I would not enjoy the long periods of manual data entry involved in the job I had interviewed for. They felt I would be better suited to another job that I didn't even know about, which was an AVA (Audio-Visual Aids) Technician. This job involved making sure that teaching staff had access to all the audio-visual equipment they might need to teach lessons – which could be a simple recording of an educational TV programme or the use of a video camera, etc.

While it was not as computer-related as I would have liked, it came with the wonderful perk of being able to enrol on any of the day-release classes that the College ran, so I got to continue learning while I was paid to work there. I chose Electronics and Electrical Engineering. I really enjoyed learning about the electronics involved in logic circuits and computers – but not so much the heavy current electrical stuff and associated mathematics.

While working at the College, an opportunity arose to do some part-time teaching of Computer Studies. I jumped at the chance even though I was barely older than the 16–18-year-old students I would be teaching, as I really liked the idea of developing ways of helping people to have fun and therefore learn more quickly. I was inspired in this direction by one of my College Tutors, Jan Howard, whose lectures I had always really enjoyed. He had a humorous and quirky way of bringing the learning to life with wacky and far-fetched examples which appealed to me greatly.

Armed with more youthful energy than experience, I began to teach. I found that the students warmed to me quickly after initially being sceptical of my abilities. We had lots of fun together learning the basics of Computer Studies, and I enjoyed thinking up silly examples of the application of what I was teaching, to help things stick in their minds.

In the middle of this period of working as an AVA Technician, studying Electronics and Electrical Engineering and teaching Computer Studies – all before I was 20 – another opportunity came up!
Mike Booth, a church friend who was an incredibly intelligent Electronics and Software Engineer and Programmer (I still aspire to be half as clever as he is) told me about a project he was working on. He was designing a data-logging computer to record the energy efficiency of housing stock on a special estate in the new city of Milton Keynes called the Energy Park, where all the houses would be more energy-efficient than normal. It was a single-board system that had quite a few inputs to record electricity and gas consumption, heating system parameters, and temperatures and humidities in various parts of a given house. Mike told me he needed help with testing some of his designs and asked if I would like to assist in some of my spare time – which I did.

After some months of helping Mike, he let me know that Milton Keynes Development Corporation were creating a job to work on the Energy Park. The role would involve installing the data-logging computers he had created in a selection of houses and attaching them to a network that spanned the whole Energy Park. Across this network the data from each house was fed back to a monitoring centre. While there was no guarantee that I would get the job, I figured that I had a good chance as I had already worked with the data-loggers while helping Mike out.

Sure enough I got the job, and started at the Energy Park almost three years to the day after starting at the College. I successfully persuaded my new employer to allow me to continue my studies, so I was getting paid for a full week, but working only four days and attending College on the fifth!

There was lots of variety in my role, and I found I enjoyed the 'social' interactions with residents just as much as the technical work itself.

Two years into the job, it was going well, and all the houses were now producing the data we needed - but I missed interacting with a wide variety of people, like the residents of the Energy Park, or the students I had taught while at the College.

I began to look around for job opportunities and was offered a potentially exciting role that a local resident had told me about, working in a Government Communication Office. I turned it down because they would not allow me to continue my day-release classes.

One of the jobs I saw in the local paper grabbed my attention. It was working as an Instructor for the Civil Aviation Authority. Teaching the maintenance and repair of systems used in airports and Air Traffic Control Centres sounded amazingly exciting, and the pay was excellent, but I thought it was the kind of job I would never get in a million years, and so I didn't bother applying.

I carried on looking for jobs, not really discontent in my position at the Energy Park but feeling there was probably more to learn.

In parallel with work, I had been advancing my interest in Radio Communications by experimenting with small transmitters. Building the actual electronic circuits and the antennae was lots of fun. I was also interested in Audio equipment, and putting it all together, I started getting into low power Pirate Radio.

One Sunday afternoon in my hometown, while out for a walk, I bumped into Ed Joinson (see, I told you he'd show up later! He was the Vice Principal at the College who gave me the AVA Technician job). Ed had moved on from the College while I was still working there, and we had not really been in touch. He asked me what I was doing workwise and listened as I explained what I did at the Energy Park. Then he said something like "...but where is it all going?". That was exactly what I had been wondering...

Ed was now working at a College of Telecoms Engineering for NATS (National Air Traffic Services). When I explained that I had done some teaching at the College after he left, he mentioned that there might be a vacancy in the Comms Group for an Instructor. It turned out that NATS was connected to the Civil Aviation Authority! This was the very job I had seen in the local paper and ruled myself out for – I could hardly believe it!

Ed connected me with the Personnel Department at the NATS College of Telecoms Engineering, and I was offered an interview for the position of Instructor in the Comms Group. The next step was to be a test lecture, where I would present to the other Instructors already working there, which I found a bit scary.

I decided to create a session on the 'Technical Problems associated with running a Pirate Radio Station'. With hindsight, this was probably not the best choice of subject matter! I practiced the lecture many times and was convinced that it contained the right level of technical information, and a nice mix of overview and detail. The day of the lecture came, and because I had spent so much time practicing, I thought I delivered the lecture reasonably well, given the pressure I felt trying to teach people who already lectured for a living.

The time for feedback came and I only really remember two things: 1) that what I had done was good enough to get the job, but 2) that Pirate Radio could interfere with Aviation Radio signals - and I'd better not continue my involvement with it!
This proved to be an extraordinary job, and I did it for nearly seven years. It was so exciting to be working behind the scenes in Airports (especially in Control Towers and going 'air side' to inspect systems near the actual runways) and Air Traffic Control Centres, and so fundamental for all the things I have done since. The training was excellent and since everything we did was mission critical, we had to do everything right – so there were not the financial pressures and pushing for short cuts that one might have found in the commercial sector.

I could go on through my CV, but the point I want to make is that the theme in this story is this: I have been very blessed that in each step of my career, someone saw something in me that I did not see in myself.

In fact, Ed Joinson made just that point in response to an email I sent, thanking him for helping me on my way in my career. He said: "It has always been one of my motivations to support and encourage anyone who I consider to be capable of more than they realise, and your career reflects this view. I certainly remember thinking that you were under-appreciated at the College and at our chance meeting in Winslow High Street."

What a blessing that Ed saw something in me I could not see in myself.

I became aware that I knew a number of people who, although technically very competent, did not achieve the level of success that I thought they should, given the technical skills they had. This seemed to me to have been because they were sadly not willing or able to communicate their value to others.

As I write this and look back over my career to date, every job I've had (when I used to interview for jobs) from the CAA/NATS Trainer role onwards has been the result of doing a presentation.
Every role I have been offered (without seeking it), including my favourite, being the Worldwide Community Director for the Asterisk Open Source project, has been the result of people seeing me do presentations.

And now pretty much every paid speaking opportunity that comes my way is the result of someone seeing me speak.
I don't mention these things to impress you, but to impress upon you the importance of being a Nerd that gets heard!

Enough about me! Now, back to you...
The very fact that you are reading this book tells me you have potential – probably more than you can possibly imagine!

And I want to be the one that helps you see it for yourself. I want to be the one that turbo-charges your career and your life by helping you be the most powerful and effective communicator and presenter you can! I want to be the one to help you truly shine!

What follows in this book is a step-by-step guide that, when you implement the protocols I identify and explain, will see you presenting in such a way that your colleagues, customers or competitors will be wowed by your abilities...
They will learn from you, be drawn to you, and remember you. You will be at the top of their mind when they are thinking of people with your specialisation!

Are you ready for the journey? Strap in – let's go!

PURPOSE

PLAN

PREFERENCES

PRACTICE

PARTICIPATION

PERFORMANCE

POSTEVENT

Chapter Two - Introduction to the Seven Power Presenting Protocols

The chapters after this one will give depth and detail about each of the individual power presenting protocols, but it is important to look at them in overview first, so that we can understand what each one does and why it is important.

Purpose

It may seem like a statement of the obvious that any and every presentation should have a purpose. However, the truth of the matter is that out of the millions of presentations that are given every day, one would be hard pressed to find a situation in which both the presenter and the audience are totally clear (and agreed) on what the purpose, or the desired outcome, really is.

The chances are that if you dropped in on any given presentation and asked the presenter and each audience member in isolation to give you the purpose of what they were going through, several different responses would be forthcoming.

And so, the Purpose protocol is not only about the presenter being crystal clear on the desired outcomes for the presentation, but that those outcomes are both communicated with, and agreed by, the audience (as early in the process of creating the presentation as possible) AND the sponsor - the person who asked you to create the presentation in the first place.

Agreeing the purpose in terms of the desired outcomes with the audience and the sponsor ensures that the creation of the presentation is heading in the right direction from the outset, and there will not be any unpleasant surprises when the time of delivery comes around - because the presentation will be on target, in terms of addressing the needs of the audience and the desired outcomes specified by the sponsor (if there is one).

In a typical scenario, the sponsor will ask you to deliver a presentation for reasons that are important to them at a business level. An example might be 'Reduce the number of tech support calls and emails for product X by 25%.'. The outcome that the sponsor is looking for often contributes to achieving one of their strategic goals.
When the purpose (in other words the desired outcomes) of the presentation has been agreed with the sponsor, it is important to test them out with your audience, or at least a representative of your audience, at the earliest possible opportunity.

Alignment between the outcomes the sponsor wants to achieve, and the needs of the audience is crucial. Establishing alignment is a foundational step and serves to establish your communications channel with the audience at the outset. This channel is necessary to allow interactions during the whole process of creating the presentation as and when required.

It will ensure maximum effectiveness of your presentation and endear you to both the sponsor and the audience. When the sponsor and the audience feel that you and they have a common goal, they are more likely to feel open and sympathetic to what you are trying to convey to them. They will be more receptive to your message if it feels like you are preaching to the choir to begin with.

The Purpose protocol is the rudder of your presentation. It is therefore of crucial importance to have this defined and agreed before you set off on your journey through the rest of the protocols, otherwise you may drift off in the wrong direction!

Plan

With the purpose of the presentation now established and agreed with the sponsor and the audience, we can set about the task of creating a structure for the presentation which will take advantage of the human attention span and various ways to get the important information in your presentation into the minds and memories of your audience.

The Plan protocol is all about generating a logical flow that will make the presentation easy and natural for you to deliver, and therefore easy and natural for your audience to receive, digest and implement.

Sadly, all too often, when technical people are asked to deliver a presentation, their minds quickly turn to a set of PowerPoint (or Keynote or Prezi, etc.) slides - without ever thinking deeply about the purpose of the presentation or how to construct it for maximum effectiveness.
But that's not us! We have already spent time considering and agreeing the purpose of our presentation with everyone that matters, and now we must devote ourselves to creating the most effective possible structure within which to deliver it.

Can you imagine how haphazard a presentation would be (and sadly many are) when the subject of a logical and easy to follow structure is never really given any consideration by the person creating the presentation?

While we do not need to be overly prescriptive and plan things down to the second, spending time considering the overall structure of our presentation, and the way we organise the material we wish to deliver within that presentation, will be of massive benefit to us, to our audience, and to our sponsor – in other words, to the overall effectiveness of the presentation.

The clarity we obtain from having a well-defined purpose for our presentation will be multiplied by the clarity and confidence we get from knowing that the information we wish to convey will be delivered in an easy to absorb way within a meaningful and thoughtfully constructed framework.

We serve our audience best when we put time into planning our presentation properly. Our communication will be boosted by having a structure that resonates with them, and the key information will be delivered in such a way that it makes the presentation a joy for you to deliver, and for them to participate in.

Preferences

Would it shock you to learn that the vast majority of presentations are conceived and delivered without any thought being given to the type of 'learners' that the audience will be made up of?

And yet nothing could be more important in terms of truly making a great connection with your audience and serving them in a way that they are most at home with.

The reason that this aspect is often omitted from the preparation that people do when they are creating a presentation, is that many of us don't have the level of self-awareness to even consciously consider our own learning styles and leanings, and this is where it all starts.

Considering our own preferences is key to then moving on to consider the preferences of others in our lives, whether that is a spouse, a colleague or (in this case) the people in your audience.

While we may have feelings of discomfort without really knowing why when there is a clash of styles, if we intentionally consider them (learning styles, both ours and those of our audience) when we are preparing our presentation, we are setting ourselves up for an altogether better experience for everyone concerned.
There are many ways of dissecting and cataloguing the way we work as people. You may have heard of different personality profile assessments like MBTI (the Myers-Briggs Type Indicator), DISC profiling or the Clifton Strengths Finder. All of these are very interesting and valid ways of assessing personality types, but for our purposes in the chapter on the Preferences protocol, we

will use a simpler tool to highlight the different ways that people like to learn.

Thinking about the preferences or learning styles of the people in our audience is yet another way of ensuring we have the greatest possible connection with them, to facilitate both the giving and receiving of information as part of the presentation.

When done properly, this will massively enhance the audience's experience, and while they may not understand why, they will feel a great resonance with you and will more easily absorb the information and feelings that you wish to pass on.

Conversely, your audience may not consciously perceive that something is off. But we can be sure that they will not get the most from your presentation if it is delivered in a way that does not consider their learning style preferences, because then we will not build experiences to make use of the way that they prefer to receive, digest and implement new information.

Practise

You may ask yourself, why is one of the protocols, and therefore an entire chapter of this book, devoted to practicing the presentation?

The answer is simple! Most people do not practise their presentation (and this is very evident when you see presenters looking a bit baffled during their own presentation, losing their place or getting ahead of themselves compared with the slides they are using).

Of the small proportion of people who do take time to practise their presentation, the kind of 'practise' they do is often inadequate and can, in some circumstances, do more harm than good.

Therefore, the point of devoting an entire chapter of this book to the benefits and practice of practise is to give you all the information you need as to why you should be practicing, and to give you the detail of the how, when, and to whom your practise should be directed.

Practise is all about building familiarity. Familiarity with the structure of your presentation, familiarity with the content of your presentation and familiarity with the cadence or the flow of your presentation.

It should therefore be seen as a process rather than a one and done kind of thing.

This means that you can begin to practice as soon as you have even just the kernel of an idea for your presentation, so long as that kernel is based on the Purpose protocol where you have defined and agreed the outcomes that you, the audience and your sponsor all want to achieve.

Often you will find that in practicing as early as possible in the development of a presentation, it will be instrumental in changing and optimising many aspects of it – from words, phrases and ideas, all the way through to the fundamental concepts you want to get across.

In short, the art of practising your presentation (however little of it you have at any point in time) is actually a part of the process of creation and perfection, rather than an activity you do after you feel your presentation is 'ready'.

There are many very practical results that come from investing time in practising. You will learn which words and phrases sounded better in your head than they do out loud. Things that made sense when you thought of them might not sound so good when you explain them to a practice audience, and you'll get a very good idea of how long your presentation lasts (which is a vital thing to know).

Lastly, when you practise with your target audience in mind, you can run the parallel process in your mind of trying to analyse how your presentation will 'land' with them; anything they may disagree with or anything that might not be appropriate for them, in terms of technical level.

By focusing your mind on your target audience, you are flexing your connection muscle, which will increase the potency and engagement of your presentation when you are in front of them.

Participation

Have you ever felt that you are having something done to you or at you that should really have been done with you?

That is the kind of uncomfortable feeling (likely accompanied by a feeling of boredom or preoccupation with something else) that can come across your audience if they do not feel engaged with you during your presentation.

And the key to engagement is participation!

Participation is crucial to any presentation, and whether it is done with questions, showing of hands, sharing of stories or whatever, it will make the whole experience feel more like a friendly conversation for them, as opposed to being on the receiving end of some kind of opaque monologue.

If you have already taken the following steps:

1) Agreed the Purpose of your presentation with the audience

2) Created a tailored-for-them plan for your presentation using a clear structure
3) Considered your audience's learning style(s) and preferences
4) Practised multiple times, with your audience in mind

...Can you see that you are already on the way to connecting with your audience and delivering a presentation so appropriate for them (in both content and style) that it will stand out to them, head and shoulders above anything else they've seen?

You can? Good!
Here's the next step: Think about ways you can involve them in the presentation, preferably that make things a bit more fun and friendly.

This is so important because of a simple equation that many presenters seem all-to-easily to forget:
INVOLVEMENT = COMMITMENT

The more you can involve your audience in any session you run, the more committed they will be to the outcomes you shared with them when working on the Purpose protocol. Of course, there will already be a level of commitment to those outcomes if you have been able to agree with the audience ahead of the presentation – and this means that you can use the presentation to support and explain the reasoning behind those outcomes, as well as showing how they can be achieved.

If you've not been able to agree on the outcomes with your audience before you meet them, then your first job is to share those outcomes with them at the beginning of your presentation and look for agreement. That is the first involvement (or micro-commitment) that your audience will participate in and will therefore help them to understand that your presentation is going to be delivered for them and with them.
They are a part of it, and feel involved in its creation, rather than merely being on the receiving end of something with a forgone conclusion.

Performance
Of course, the activity of actually delivering your presentation is of critical importance, and you need to feel as prepared and confident as you can be in the given set of circumstances.
But YOU are in control of many of the factors that contribute to those circumstances – and are therefore in a pivotal position to form the circumstances!

For example, you are in control of establishing the purpose of your presentation, in terms of desired outcomes, and then sharing and agreeing them with your audience.

You are in control of the level of work you put into the structure of your presentation, how much participation you have designed in, and the amount of practise you have done (amongst many other aspects of your preparations). Therefore, you are largely in control of the level of confidence, clarity and composure you will feel as you ready yourself to step out and actually deliver your presentation to your intended audience.

What I am saying here is that YOU can give yourself a flying start to being a position where the stresses of delivering your presentation are minimised.

And your audience are looking for a few different things from you – high on the list after relevant subject matter knowledge and/or experience will be the confidence of your delivery (this will be perceived as your confidence in your message), your ability to help your audience feel at ease and a part of the experience of your presentation, and some entertainment value.

All of these things can be made or broken by your performance, and so the Performance protocol is there to help you build on the platform of your excellent preparations to deliver your presentation with so much confidence and clarity that it is a pleasure for your audience.

This really goes without saying, but I'm going to say it anyway…

If there are two people with equal subject matter expertise and experience, and one makes the effort to up his presentation game in terms of preparation, delivery style and engagement, then we all know which one will get the job, make the sale, have their advice heeded or be remembered for when their services are required.

The more you can optimise the performance aspect of your presentation, the deeper and longer-lasting the connection you will have with your audience – and the more aligned they will feel with your message.

Post-Event

Can you imagine delivering presentation that resonates really powerfully with your audience and convinces them that a certain change needs to be made, a course of action needs to be taken, or a product/service needs to be purchased – only to lose the opportunity to do business or see your ideas bear fruit, all because you didn't follow up properly after the presentation?

This is exactly what happens time and time again in the real world, and I will explain why!

You've probably heard your Sales colleagues say, 'The fortune is in the follow-up', and it's totally true. Making a presentation or giving a demo is only one part of a larger chain of events that have desired outcomes at several different levels.

And yet all too often the 'drive-by' presentation is a fact of life for many presenters and audiences alike.

A 'drive-by' presentation is one where the presenter does not consult with the audience in the lead up to the presentation being delivered, nor during the presentation at any meaningful level. This is a recipe for a poor presentation in terms of the relevance of content and can leave audiences feeling frustrated or even disenfranchised.

The problem is compounded by a lack of follow-up after the presentation, and by follow-up I mean more than just a post-presentation survey or Q&A session (although both of these have their place).

The great news is that you are not a 'drive-by' presenter if you have worked through the first six Power Presenting Protocols. In fact you will already be head and shoulders above most other presenters – and you can build on (rather than lose) that advantage by having an effective framework for Post-Event activities after your presentation has been delivered.

Some kind of evaluation mechanism of the presentation itself is useful in terms of being able to ascertain what participants thought of the session itself, and whether the objectives of the session were achieved.

As an example, one of the objectives of a session could be: 'Demonstrate familiarity with the five new features of version 3.0 of product X.'

No doubt the achievement (or not) of this objective could easily be measured by a practical test, a quiz or maybe a group exercise at the end of the session.
There are, however, likely to be higher level objectives in place that have led to the need for this presentation – and these will have been articulated in the Purpose protocol.

As we mentioned in the Purpose protocol, one of those higher-level objectives could be:
'Reduce the number of tech support calls and emails for product X by 25%.'

This is something that cannot be immediately measured, as those that have participated in the session need time to put their new knowledge/skills/working practices into use, and so a considered mechanism is necessary to judge whether the higher-level objective has been met – at an appropriate time after the presentation.

That mechanism is the Purpose protocol, as it provides a way of agreeing outcomes between you (the presenter), the sponsor (whoever asked you to deliver the presentation) and the audience, and can provide the timeframes in which outcomes can be measured.
In this case, you may have agreed that you will review the outcome in terms of change in number of tech support calls one month after the presentation (as this should allow enough time for participants to put their newly acquired knowledge and familiarity with the five new features of version 3.0 of product X into practice).

This review will logically lead to agreement of what the next step should be, which might be one of the following:

*Mission accomplished – no further action!
*Tech Support calls reduced by 15% - follow up with some on the job reinforcement.
*Tech Support calls reduced by 25% - deliver a modified version of the presentation to Salespeople, to help them sell more successfully.

The focus here should be an ongoing relationship to ensure your audience's and sponsor's needs are met –

they are your customers – and this will help inform future presentations, so that they are even more ‘on target’.

Now that we know the “what”, and have some understanding of the “why”, let us discover the “how”…

Chapter Three -
Protocol 1: Purpose

What is the purpose of your presentation? This may seem like an obvious question, but you must be absolutely clear what the answer is before you make a start. Otherwise, you will be looking at a whole lot of wasted effort. It's a bit like answering an exam question. You may have plenty of interesting information to tell the examiner, but if you are not actually answering the question asked, you score zero.

Is it your intention to educate, to inform, or to entertain? All these outcomes are good, and what I have found is that when you build in entertainment and fun, then more of the desired outcomes will be obtained. In fact, you may have heard the new word "edutainment". This captures the idea of both educating and entertaining people at the same time - which is a very effective thing to do. While it is useful to keep in mind different modes of presenting, we need to seriously consider both the aims and objectives of any presentation we are going to make.

Let's start by thinking about the aims. These are the general outcomes that we are looking for. For example, we may say that the aim of the presentation is to familiarise people with the new operating procedure, or another aim may be for people to start using the new CRM system.

SMART objectives

The objectives, on the other hand, are more about the specific things that we are looking to achieve during this presentation. You have probably heard the acronym, "SMART", used to describe objectives, whether those objectives are for a presentation, or in terms of personal goals within the workplace setting. So, let's go through what "SMART" means.

"S" stands for "specific"; you need to be able to pinpoint the outcome you are looking for. It's no good just saying "I want to change my weight". That could mean the speaker wants to lose weight or put it on. If the real objective is to lose weight, we need to be specific in order to communicate that.

"M" is for "measurable". You've perhaps heard it said, "If you can't measure it, you can't manage it". We need to be able to know when we have achieved our objective, and that's where the measurement aspect comes in. For example, saying "I want to lose weight" is a good start, however, it would be good to specify either the amount of weight I want to lose, or the target weight I'm looking to achieve, because, in doing either of those things, I add a measurable element to the objectives.

The "A" in "SMART" stands for "agreed" or "accepted". When I'm setting objectives for a presentation, it will be an uphill struggle if these are not shared by the audience, if they feel they can't achieve them, or if they don't understand them. It is important to create straightforward objectives that are understood and aimed for by both the presenter and the audience.

"R" is for realistic. In other words, it is not profitable to cook up an objective if it is simply beyond our current capabilities. Now, I'm not saying that we should not have stretch goals, and that we should not set ourselves objectives that seem challenging for us to achieve – no. What I'm saying here is that it must be humanly possible. For instance, it would be useless to create an objective that said "I want to lose 30 pounds in one week" because that's really beyond the bounds of human ability.

The "T" in "SMART" objectives stands for "time-bound". It is essential to place a timeline on the objective. If we never set it against a date or time, then we will not be compelled to achieve it. Having a generalised desire or goal is likely to amount to nothing if we do not act upon it with the imperative of a deadline. Once you have set a deadline, you can decide upon mini milestones and then work backwards from there. Continuing the weight example: if someone were to desire to lose 30 pounds in six months, they could say, "By the end of the first month,

I want to have lost 5 pounds." It is also in some people's nature to work much better and more diligently when there is a deadline imposed.

To put all this together into an example of a "SMART" objective:

"I wish to lose 30 pounds in weight, within the next six months."
I think we can agree that this is a specific, measurable, agreed or accepted, realistic, time-bound objective.

Now, let's address the stakeholders in a presentation. You may ask – who are the stakeholders? Well, the stakeholders that I identify in any given presentation are the sponsor, the presenter and the audience.

The sponsor is the person that has commissioned the presentation. There will be a person who has asked you to deliver the presentation for some reason; maybe they are paying you, maybe they have an agenda of their own, and so the onus is on you to talk with the sponsor and to agree the aims and objectives. This will link the two of you, thus two of the three stakeholders will be joined together in agreeing the outcomes for the presentation at an early stage. This is best done, I believe, by agreeing on some overall aims and some very specific objectives that the two of you are tied into.

As the presenter, you really want to do your best for the sponsor. You want to accomplish the things that they are looking to achieve, and you want to deliver the outcomes that they've asked you to deliver. Of course, you also want to build a relationship with that sponsor, so that you might be asked to do more presentations for them, or to deliver more outcomes for them. If you're the kind of person that's keen to get things right the first time (as we all are, in terms of delivering a presentation), then it's important that you liaise with that sponsor and set some objectives with them.

You could sit down across the table from them and go through the objectives - that would be a great idea if you can get an appointment with them in the time frame that you're looking to. Or, another way of doing it would be to create the aims and objectives yourself and send it over to them as a strawman document (an initial draft of the kind of things you're thinking), and let them modify it.

I have found over many years of experience that this is the best way to get things moving out fast. As long as you request that they send you some objectives, you'll probably find that you're asking them repeatedly, and they never really get round to it; but, if you set the objectives - even in draft form - and send them over to the sponsor, then they'll soon come back to you and say, "Oh yes, generally you're right, but we need to tweak this particular objective", or, "You've missed something and I would like to add this" etc. This will be great practice for you to be aligned with the sponsor at the earliest possible opportunity.

Let's talk about the situation where you have now agreed the aim and objectives with the sponsor. So, that's the two of you aligned, but of course we have the third stakeholder, which is the audience. The objectives certainly need to be agreed with them, and therefore it is very good practice to go through the objectives of a presentation at the beginning, with the audience, and to get them to agree with or buy into those very objectives.

Here is an example of how I would do this. After I've opened up the presentation and told them the title and the reason for it etc. in general terms, I present an overall aim. I then focus on some specific objectives. There could be three objectives, five objectives or even more - but you don't want the number to be too big, so as to avoid overwhelming the audience. I usually start with a phrase like "by the end of the presentation, you will be able to…" and then go on to state the objectives.

The first objective may be "to list the three options that exist for entering data onto the new system"; another objective may be "demonstrate familiarity with the new procedure on how to add patients to the system" and so forth. After I have presented the aim(s) and objectives, I will ask the audience how they feel about them and whether I have missed anything, at which point most will just nod and accept your ideas.

There may be an audience member that contributes another objective, which is great, or one may comment that a certain objective is not necessary. In this case, you are at liberty to agree and omit the objective, or you may mention that it was requested by management etc. and so needs to be addressed.

Having carried this out, the aim is that all three stakeholders (sponsor, presenter and audience) are locked into these objectives and the desires and needs of each party are considered and addressed in the process of agreeing them.

Another thing to be mindful of is the time frame – when are they going to be able to use the skills and knowledge you will transmit to them in the presentation? It would be foolish to try and train them in a skill if they are not going to use the skill until the next year or two, or if you attempted to give them some important information that they could not make use of until a new system is installed in several months' time. In other words, the presentation must be timely, and this is something to bear in mind when agreeing the aims and objectives with the sponsor, ensuring your presentation will be of maximum benefit to their current needs.

So, we've talked about the agreeing purpose of the presentation in terms of its aims and objectives. Now what we do, bearing all the above in mind, is document this in an outcome agreement. This only needs to be a few short lines in an email, which can be circulated/iterated until everyone is happy.

Example Outcome Agreement

Share something like this initially, and iterate until there is agreement:

Product X version 3.0 Presentation

Presentation Aim: To familiarise participants with version 3.0 of Product X

Presentation Objectives: By the end of the session participants will be able to:

- (a) List three advantages of version 3.0
- (b) Demonstrate familiarity with the installation process for version 3.0
- © Demonstrate familiarity with the upgrade process for version 3.0
- (d) State the 5 most important features of version 3.0

Presentation effectiveness measurement:

- (a) Participant quiz at the end of the session

(b) Participant feedback survey at the end of the session

Business Aims / Objectives:

(a) Reduce technical support enquiries on Product X version 3.0 by 35%, compared to previous versions

Presentation effectiveness in terms of Business Aims / Objectives measurement:

(a) Tech Support Manager to report enquiry volumes one month after launch of Product X version 3.0
(b) Survey of participants on how well the presentation equipped them to support Product X version 3.0 one month after launch

Presenter:	David Duffett
Sponsor:	Clayton Farlow, Tech Support Manager
Audience Reps:	Pete / Engineering, Ian / Support, Jenny / Customer Success

Note that this example does not specify a duration for the session, as this will be a function of when the outcomes have been agreed, which in turn will dictate the content, which will determine the duration.

The purpose of the outcome agreement is to explicitly sign up the three stakeholders to the outcomes for the presentation, and this means we're leaving no room for ambiguity. This also means that we've got an audit trail that we can refer to in any case of misunderstanding. This outcome agreement can be used at both the beginning and the end of the presentation. At the beginning we can use it to highlight the agreed outcomes.

We have already gained agreement with the sponsor, but we want to gain agreement with the audience at the start of the presentation (if we have not been able to do so in advance, during our prep.), so the aims and objectives are understood by all. By revisiting the outcome agreement at the conclusion of the presentation, we go back to the objectives to check that we've actually achieved those - since they form a handy checklist of the things we were looking to accomplish.

It is important to create a very clear outcome agreement, writing the general aim and individual objectives plainly. With this however, we do still want to allow for modifications, so that each party feels a sense of ownership – as mentioned above, "involvement = commitment." If they are involved in specifying the objectives, then they are more likely to be committed to achieving them.

Assuming you know the subject matter well enough to deliver on the agreed objectives, implementing this protocol will guarantee success, leaving both your audience and your sponsor delighted and united in their agreement on your achievement. 😊

Chapter Four -
Protocol 2: Plan

It is essential to plan any presentation that you are going to give. When we fail to plan, we plan to fail. However, if you put in the requisite amount of work, then you will create a presentation that is easy for you to deliver - and if it's easy for you to deliver, it will be easy for your audience to receive.

Imagine what it would be like if you were on trial for something truly terrible, perhaps some heinous crime you did not commit, and somehow, things have reached the point where you're summoned to appear in court and have acquired legal representation. As the court date approaches, you ask your attorney how the case they're preparing for you is going, to which they respond, "Actually, I find it's easier if I just wing it, you know! I'll just see how it comes to me at the time." You'd be horrified, wouldn't you? This is the case for presenters who do not plan – the results are usually horrifying!

Planning with Structure

Great presentations always have a structure to them, and the structure typically used is the good old one: beginning, middle and end. It's very important to have that structure, because it will allow people to follow the logical flow of your presentation. The other reason it's vital, is that the beginning and ending are the parts most people remember. For instance, you probably remember your first day in a given job and your last day in that job, but you don't necessarily remember all the days in between. You probably remember the beginning of a film and the end of the film, but you may not remember the full contents of the film - and so the beginning and the end of a presentation are what we refer to as Prime Time. This is your key opportunity to get the main message into your audience's minds and maybe hearts.

If you watch a news programme, you will notice that they have the headlines first (the beginning), then they give you the stories behind the headlines (the middle), and subsequently they finish by summarising the headlines (the end). In other words, they get three attempts at giving you the key information. So it is with a good presentation. You'll get three attempts: three places to impart your information. This is crucial, because the attention span of any given audience is not necessarily going to be very long at all. Thus, it is important to grab and maintain their attention by leading your audience through a presentation with a well-thought-out structure that is logical and easy to digest for them.

Timings

Now, you may be wondering what to do about timing the various sections of your presentation. To give you a very rough idea: if your presentation was, say, thirty minutes, you might spend around three minutes on the introduction, approximately twenty-four minutes on the main body of the presentation, and then another three-ish minutes at the end of the presentation, summarising it. Here is a diagrammatic representation of what your overall structure might look like

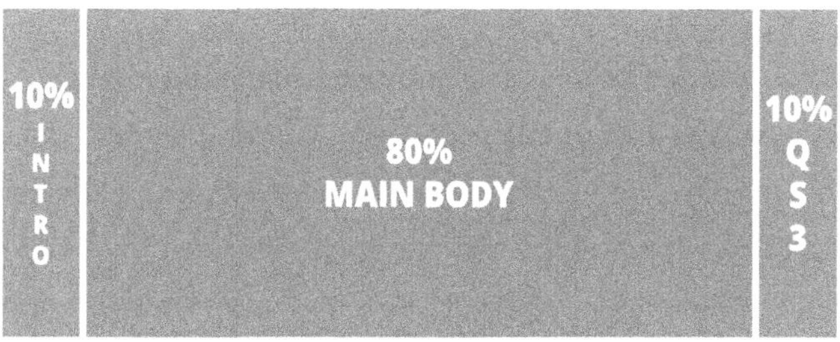

Figure 1. An example of the overall structure

We'll think more about how to construct each section of the structure effectively next...

The Beginning

The beginning of your presentation is the most important part (the end is a very, very close second – more on that later) and so we need to invest time and effort into making it as attention-grabbing and effect as possible.

Not only are we in "you never get a second chance to make a first impression" territory, but this is the perfect time to demonstrate to our audience exactly why they should listen to us, in terms of the relevance of our message to them and the outcomes they can expect.

Our first job is to break any pre-occupations they may have (checking their email, chatting with their neighbours, any problems on their mind) and, with that done, we must grab them by the throat, metaphorically, and then draw them in to our presentation, demonstrating that it is best use of their time for the coming 25, 30, whatever minutes (I would suggest never longer than 40 minutes in a single sitting).

People love order and sequence when hearing new information, learning new things, etc. so we can also use the beginning of our presentation to set our audience up to expect a logical flow in what we are going to share with them. This lets them know that we have put a lot of work into choosing and refining a sequence to what we are doing, and it introduces them to the topic and our main points too.

Further, we can give guidelines at the beginning of our presentation on anything we want, like how we would prefer to deal with questions (e.g. as we go along or maybe nearer the end).

We can prepare our audience to expect interaction, or ask them to think of experiences or stories they can share later.

The beginning and ending of our presentation really is our 'prime time' to do a number of important things.
In a few pages time, you'll meet my acronym PROOF, where P stands for primacy (the beginning) and R stands for recency (the ending) of the presentation – these are key parts that we simply must ensure are the best they can be.

Another name for the beginning of our presentation is the introduction, and I have a useful 'INTRO' mnemonic that acts as a guide to the component part of a great introduction (I am not prescribing that you must always include all of these five elements, but they should all certainly be considered for each presentation or demo you work on):

Impact: The very first thing you say or do should grab the attention of the audience and draw them into your presentation.

Need: You must then explain why the audience needs to take notice of this presentation.

Title: At this point, you may stress the title of your presentation, which should lock into the minds of your audience the purpose of what you're presenting.

Range: Tell the audience the various things you plan to cover in the presentation, in a logical and concise way.

Objectives: This is the time to state that aim and those objectives we've just spoken about in the last chapter! This will clearly outline what it is you want the audience to achieve.

Additionally, depending on the nature of your presentation, "Q" may be added to the end, for:

Questions: Express whether you want your audience to ask questions during the presentation, as they come to mind, or hold them until near the end.

Thinking about Impact, this is the device you use to grab the audiences' attention at the outset. Some examples might be:
A thought-provoking question
A fascinating fact
A stunning statistic
A humorous quote or maxim

When it comes to articulating why your audience Needs to give you their time and attention, this must be done in terms of benefits for them, ideally identifying what they will get in terms of business advantages and then going beyond those and into how it will improve their personal lives.
Of course, to know the outcomes people are looking for, you need to have been in touch with them, consulted with them and agreed those outcomes (which is exactly what we did in the Purpose protocol).

Having a crisp, punchy, humorous or intriguing Title will really crystalise what your talk is about and give people an anchor when thinking about it and/or mentioning to people afterwards.
Coming up with such a title can be challenging, and this is a great opportunity to use your favourite AI helper to suggest a few ideas after you properly brief it about the nature of your talk, the target audience, etc.

Outlining the Range of what you are going to cover achieves at least two things; it gives people your key information (your headlines) right at the beginning of your time, when they are most attentive AND it pre-programmes them to expect a predictable and logic flow to what you are going to share. In the age-old language of presentation skills training from years gone by, you are telling them what you are going to tell them!

Sharing your Objectives also helps your audience to understand what you are going to achieve together, and acts as a guide to the (agreed, if you've been through the Purpose protocol) outcomes you're heading towards. These may be as high-level or as detailed as you want them to be and/or as your audience needs them to be. Measurability is a key aspect to consider

Your Question policy is a choice you can make, as the presenter, based on the contents of the presentation you're giving. Sometimes, it's great to let people ask questions any time as this gives them the satisfaction of an immediate answer (Just-in-Time Learning) and prevents them being distracted by that question for the remainder of the presentation. At other times, however, if you have a shorter amount of time or you want to give the presentation in a logical and uninterrupted flow, you may want to let the audience know that questions will be addressed at the end (prior to the summary), or even after the presentation (if absolutely necessary – this is least preferable), in which case you can encourage people to write them down so that they do not forget them. Remember: as the presenter – you are in charge!

The Middle

Now we come to the middle. This is the main body and content of the presentation and, although vitally important, is often the section that is most neglected in planning. Many an audience member has found themselves lost while in the middle of a presentation – perhaps it has even happened to you.

When people lose the thread of the presentation, they will turn their attention to something else: maybe what they're going to have for lunch or dinner, maybe something a little more active like checking their emails or social media. Whatever it is, they will find a way to distract themselves from the boredom and frustration of being on the receiving end of a presentation that they can no longer follow. The good news is that this does not have to be the case with your presentation! Not only can we help with ways to impact and access the audience's memory with your content, but also with planning tools and techniques to develop a full body of content for your presentation.

Content Planning Tools and Techniques

Whilst there are a huge number of ways you could plan the content of your presentation; the people I teach in my Masterclasses have found these two ways to be most effective:

The "Top Down" Method

The "Top Down" method is simple. You just pick the most important headings (ideally three) about your topic and then make a number of points (possibly three 😉) inside each of those headings. If we were talking about road safety, our three headings might be:

1. Road Safety by the Numbers
2. Factors Affecting Road Safety
3. Your Part in Making Roads Safer

Within these three headings, we pick three points to make in support of them:

1. Road Safety by the Numbers
    a. Statistics from previous years and trends
    b. The current situation
    c. Five-year forecast
2. Factors Affecting Road Safety
    a. The changing nature of road users
    b. Technology and, in particular, driverless cars
    c. Highway design
3. Your Part in Making Roads Safer

a. Awareness of the greatest dangers
b. Your road use
c. Passing on good advice/Outreach

This is a great way of both identifying the content of your presentation and creating the structure at the same time.

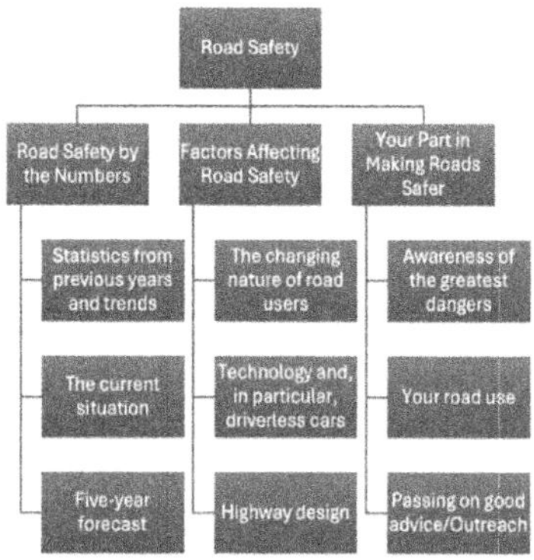

Figure 2. The top down approach

An extension of the "Top Down" approach is the Mind Map. For some, creating a Mind Map (also known as a Spider Diagram) may feel more creative and free-flowing due to its visual nature. If you've not come across the concept of Mind Maps before, they're very straightforward. Take a sheet of paper and write your main topic or talk title right in the middle of it, then draw a circle around it. You then draw a line out from that title for each main point you want to make, and draw mini

branches of that line for the sub-points that support the main point.
Take a look at this example.

Figure 3. Example mind map

Beware! Both the Top Down and Mind Map approaches carry the risk of missing something if it does not flow from the main headings you've come up with first, so this is something you need to bear in mind when using these planning techniques.

The "Bottom Up" Method
Another way of putting a plan together for the content you wish to cover is the "Bottom Up" approach.The "Bottom Up" method involves using scraps of paper or Post-Its™ to note down each individual idea as you brainstorm every aspect you can think of around your overall topic. You just write one aspect or item per Post-It™.

Once you have run out of things to put on the Post-It™s, you lay them all out on a table (or the floor, or a wall), step back, and take a look. You will find that a good number of them will naturally fall into groups, and when you give headings to these groups, they will emerge as one of your (three) main headings, or as sub-points.

You may also find that if you have an odd Post-It™ that does not fit into a group, you decide not to include it at all, or maybe have a section near the end of your talk when you cover 'other aspects'.

Here is an example of the Bottom Up approach.

Brainstormed ideas on Post-Its™, and Post-Its™ organised into groups

Figure 4. Example of the "bottom up" approach to content organisation

Three is Key

It is well known that there is great power in threes, and this is certainly the case in presentation. Of course, this is not set in stone, but you will have found with presentations that you've been on the receiving end of,

that main bodies which come in threes tend to stick in people's minds just that little bit better.
For example, towards the end of your powerful introduction, you might say, "I'm here to talk about Internet Security today, and my three objectives are that by the end of our session you will be able to: 1) list the threats you must secure against, 2) explain the steps to secure your Internet connection, and lastly, 3) run the tests to prove your connection is secure". You will have given your audience three significant main goals that you want them to come away having learned and accomplished, and a simple, logical set of things that you're going to achieve throughout the presentation.

Just in case you needed any more persuading, you will find the triplet is an extremely well-used technique for powerfully conveying a message, examples being Julius Caesar's "Veni, vidi, vici" (I came, I saw, I conquered), the phrase "life, liberty, and the pursuit of happiness" from the US Declaration of Independence.

It is thought that the power of three is so important because most humans can hold three things in their mind with relative ease. Beyond three things, as we tend to think of 'a few' or 'a lot'.

Use this to your advantage to deliver an impactful, insightful and influential presentation!

PROOF - Accessing the Audience's Memory

If you want your audience to remember the content you are presenting, you're going to need to give them "PROOF". Before I unfold the mnemonic, here is an illustration of it:

Imagine, if you will, that your friend wants to show you a set of 50 photos of their recent holiday to Alaska. They're itching to show you these photos, and you are itching to see them. So, you go and look at them, and afterwards you try to see which ones you remember. I would suggest to you that the ones you remember will fit into five categories. To begin with: Primacy. You are likely to remember the first few photos they showed you. The second category is Recency; the final two or three photos, you will probably be able to commit to memory also. The third category is Over-emphasis. This could be in the form of repetition, for example, if a photo of a puffin popped up every five photos, you would remember the puffin(s). The fourth category is photos which are Outstanding. For instance, if most of the photos were landscape scenes but one of them was of a very large moose riding a bicycle - that would be outstanding, and therefore it would be memorable. The final category is Familiar photos - you will remember the photos linked to something you already know or are familiar with. Say you've been on holiday recently, too, and visited a particular landmark or well-known place to eat which looked like one in a photo they'd shown you – this would tend to stick in your mind because it linked to your own experience.

Figure 5. A picture that would be truly Outstanding

So, here's the "PROOF" you need to access the audience's memory...

Primacy:	People remember the first things you show or tell them.
Recency:	People remember the last things you show or tell them.
Over-emphasis:	People remember what you share repeatedly, or with extra emphasis.
Outstanding:	People remember the unusual things within your presentation.

Familiar: People remember what relates to their existing knowledge or experience.

What we're going to do as great presenters, is use this knowledge about accessing the audience's memory to make sure we help people file away all the information we would like them to retain.
We have previously used the example of a news programme to highlight the beginning, middle and end structure, but television is also a great example of the P and R in "PROOF". Did you know that the first advertisement (primacy) immediately after a programme is more expensive than the one in the middle of the break? The last ad (recency) just before a programme begins or resumes is more expensive too! In the UK, you will find that there are ads tied to specific programmes, so each time the programme begins or goes for a break, there's an ad for that sponsor repeatedly. Some companies will even buy both the first and last ad in order to make an impression. Let's use primacy and recency to make an impression in our public speaking.

Although primacy and recency are largely about the beginning and ending of a presentation, we can implement these specific keys within the main body as well in order to access the audience's memory. The way we can do this is to create more opportunities for primacy and recency within the middle of the presentation. For example, take a short break to refresh people and give them renewed energy for the second part of your presentation. By doing this, you are creating yet another opportunity to have a beginning and an ending (of the two halves). You may say in the run-up to the break, "We're just coming up to a short interval, so remember the main points, A, B and C", and as you come in after the break, you can say, "Just before the break we spoke of A, B and C..."

If you are unable to take a break, another way might be to divide things up into smaller segments, and then each of those into mini segments. Remember – three is key! In doing so, you will maintain the attention of your audience by giving them signposts between one section and another, frequently opening and closing the various chapters and creating effective opportunities for small beginnings and endings. For example, after you've given your introduction (continuing the "Three is Key" illustration), you can then say, "Ok, first of all, let's look at the main threats you must secure your internet against". When you get to the end of that, you might say, "Right, that was the first objective - now let's move on to the second one...". In doing so, you are giving your audience signposts, which will help them logically follow along with the content of your presentation, whilst additionally creating moments of primacy and recency throughout the body of the presentation. This will help sustain an audience's attention, even outside of traditional Prime Time!

One way to use over-emphasis in your presentation is repetition. You may repeat key information again and again to encourage your audience to remember it. You may also implement over-emphasis by way of speaking a certain phrase or word louder during a sentence each time you say it, in order to push a certain idea or point home. You can see this take effect when (depending on your presentation environment) your audience begin to react to things you have been repeating or emphasising in a way that shows they have taken them on board. They might say that word or phrase in the way that you have, whilst asking a question, or they may repeat information you have given whilst giving an answer. We all remember facts or phrases that school teachers or professors used again and again, and so it is with public speaking. The audience will take away what we over-emphasise.

Although it may not always be appropriate to show a picture of a large moose riding a bicycle, it is important that your presentation has elements which are outstanding. This could be in the form of hard-hitting statistics, thought-provoking questions or experiences that create a deep impression and play well to getting your key points across. Try to ensure your outstanding aspect is relevant to your content; it is no good telling an exceptional story if it is not contributing towards the overall aim of your presentation. People will not remember even one run of the mill, uninspiring presentation, but they will certainly remember something outstanding or unusual. So, make sure there is something outstanding (in a positive way) in your presentation, and the audience will find your presentation memorable.

Lastly, be sure to include something familiar in your presentation. Using relatable illustrations when teaching or presenting is a surefire way to connect with your audience and access their memory. When people are speaking of an unfamiliar concept, it is very hard to engage unless you can link or compare it to something you already have an understanding of. There is a very straightforward formula we can use to achieve this:

"You know X? Well Y is rather like that, because Z."
E.g. You know the way water runs through a hosepipe? Well, current running
through an electrical circuit is rather like that. This is because when you put your foot on the hosepipe, you can reduce the flow of water through it, and in like manner we can introduce resistance to reduce the flow of current through the circuit.

The use of a universally familiar example makes the unfamiliar specific concept you are explaining easier to understand.
You may ask, "Why should I take the trouble to "PROOF" my presentation?"

Let's compare the results between when we do and when we don't. Planning your presentation and creating a sound structure is all about using every minute of your presentation to maximum effect. We have already mentioned that the beginning and ending of the presentation (the P and R of PROOF) are the typical Prime Time, as pictured in the following diagram...

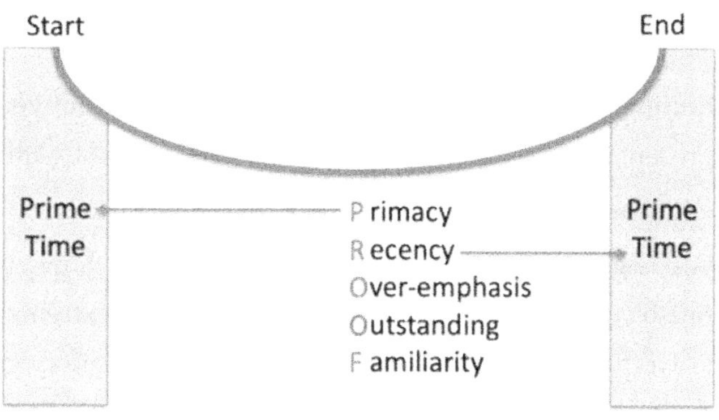

Figure 6. Putting PROOF in your presentation
You will notice that the thick line representing audience attention looks like a shallow 'U' shape – indicating that it can lull after the initial few minutes of your presentation and then go up again towards the end.

By using the above tools and techniques to produce stellar content, shaping the main body into three sections and accessing the audience's memory through your intentional planning, you are sure to create a presentation which will be captivating and entertaining whilst also being informative and influential. When you have made sure to "PROOF" your presentation, you will achieve results.

By implementing the OOF of PROOF during the main body of your presentation, you can sustain the audience's attention in an exceptional way, making your planned performance purposeful and productive.

The Ending

Endings are very, very, VERY important. You want your presentation to end with a bang and certainly not with a whimper, and so to this end - see what I did there 😉 - you're going to want to put a lot of thought into how you finish your presentation. The ending should be extremely powerful. It is the pinnacle of the entire presentation and the moment at which you should leave your audience inspired and ready to take action. You may have heard presentations that finished with an impactful quote or perhaps a thought-provoking question. However, let me ask you this: how does the average presentation that you have seen end?

Most of the time, the answer is either, "And that's it!" or, "Does anyone have any questions?"

We will further discuss the role of questions in presentations later (see Participation Protocol), but one thing I would like to stress is that you should never, ever finish your presentation with an audience Q&A. The reason for this is that when you finish that way, you are handing control to the audience to give those questions - and when the questions start to dry up (if there were any at all), then things seem to fizzle out and become flat. So, the best way to address this is to open for a short time of questions, having covered everything you wish to cover, prior to your power summary. This way, you end with the control and have directed them accordingly in a way they will recognise and appreciate throughout the presentation. Remember also that the finishing part of your presentation is the last area of Prime Time, so it needs to be used to maximum effect.

There are a number of effective endings, but one of the most compelling is the conclusion that links to the beginning. To give you an example:
Many years ago, as part of the application process for a Training Manager position, I delivered a presentation that spoke of the money spent on training for employees of U.K. companies. I had researched and found a certain industry body which had a figure for the total amount

annually spent. Although I don't remember the exact figure, for the purpose of this illustration, I happen to know that $86.7 billion was spent in the US on employee training in 2018. So, at the beginning of the presentation, I asked how much money they thought was spent on employee training each year and then allowed my small audience (there were only four or five people) to have a guess at the figure. They came out with various numbers, all of which were far below the mark. I then revealed the actual figure to their astonishment, and followed up by asking them how much of that money they thought was well spent. Of course, this figure was not known, or even easy to guess, but we all agreed that not all the money spent achieved the desired results. Having engaged their interest in the subject, I continued to the main body of my presentation. Just after I had summarised, I finished by saying, "We found out earlier that $86.7 billion is spent on training every year. That means that, as I've been speaking over the last 25 minutes, $17.4 million dollars has been spent on employee training. I want to assure you that if you appointed me as your Training Manager, your share of that money would not be wasted. Thank you!" Did I get the job? Of course, I did!

As you can see, what I did was link the end of my presentation to the intrigue I had created at the beginning. This was a powerful technique because, having drawn the audience in with an engaging question and fascinating fact, I was able to link back to the beginning, closing this chapter in their minds, whilst also reminding them of the decision in hand, i.e. to appoint me as their Training Manager.

The end of your presentation is one of the most crucial parts (arguably THE most crucial). As stated above, it's your time to summarise, let people know what the next step is, give a powerful call to action.

Never, ever, ever squander the ending of your presentation by finishing with Q&A. I suggest a little formula I call QS3 - after you get to the end of the main body of your presentation, take time to deal with any questions there might be (that's the Q), then summarise your main points (that's the S) and then finish with a powerful triple ending that either crystalises your main point, delivers your call to action or (if possible) both!

Q - Questions and answers

S - Summary of main points

3 - A powerful triple ending

Here's one of my triple endings:

"It's been a pleasure speaking with you this evening. It's been a pleasure showing you how to achieve more with your presentations. But the real pleasure will come for you when you implement these protocols and thus receive all the rewards that come from being a Nerd that gets heard! Thank you!"

So, how will you end your next presentation?

Although knowing just what to say and how to say it can be a dreaded element for many when planning a presentation, these tools will help you immeasurably. Now that you know what a good structure looks like, how to plan each section of it effectively, how to "PROOF" your presentation, and how to form the content that will supply the structure, you will be amazed at what a difference this makes! I am certain you will be even more confident for having intentionally planned your presentation, and one step closer to being a Nerd that gets heard!

Chapter Five - Protocol 3: Preferences

You are now ready to ensure that your presentation has maximum impact, by taking the time to walk in your audience's shoes. This preparation phase is not so much about the contents of your presentation, since you have now established its purpose and planned a structure. This phase is about the audience and their preferences.

What I mean by the audience's preferences is how they receive, digest and implement information. In other words, what is/are their preferred Learning Style(s)? It is so easy to default to your own preferred Learning Style when preparing a presentation because of course, this is what comes naturally to you. But you are not the audience. And because the audience is composed of several people, you can guarantee they are going to have several different preferred Learning Styles between them.

It is amazing to me that many Geeks will deliver a presentation without really thinking about who the audience is, what is important to them and how that audience will best receive and digest the information that needs to be passed on. The answers to some of these questions may be more obvious than others (especially if you have followed the previous two Protocols), and some down to your specific situation, but my aim here is to make you stop and think about your audience! When analysis of the audience is left out of preparation, the Presenter (that's you!) will almost always default to their own preferred way of doing things – and this is often a terrible mistake!

Let's take a minute or two to think about your own Learning Style. Your Learning Style is your preferred way of assimilating new information. There have been numerous studies of this dimension of human behaviour, such as Honey and Mumford's analysis, which categorised people based on four different preferences for learning: activist, pragmatist, reflector and theorist. Although there are many other well-reputed systems, I would like to boil Honey and Mumford's work down to a very simple model for our purposes here. It's called the Learning Cycle.

The Learning Cycle

The Learning Cycle has three phases: Input, Action and Reflection. In order for true learning to take place, each phase must be completed. The phases, and the relationship between them, are identified in Figure 7 below:

Figure 7. The Learning Cycle

As you can see, the three phases have a set sequence, but you can start at any one of them. Your own personal Learning Style will dictate which one you like to start at. Since there are only three phases, the only combinations are as follows:

Input > Action > Reflection
Action > Reflection > Input
Reflection > Input > Action

As mentioned earlier, a person needs to go through all three phases for learning to take place. You will have your own preference, and so will each and every member of your audience.

Let's take the example of a brand-new bean-to-cup coffee machine. Imagine you have been given one as a gift… It comes in a very nice box, along with the required accessories, leads and a very comprehensive instruction manual…

Are you the kind of person who is going to thoroughly read that manual cover to cover before you even so much as plug that coffee machine in? Probably not! This is because you're a Geek and you probably want to just dive straight in and get going with this new toy. If, when you have got it all connected up and started playing with it, you find there is something you just can't do, then you might (grudgingly) read the manual.

If this describes you, then you are an ACTION oriented person – probably like the majority of Geeks. Also, the fact that you only resort to the manual as your last source of information shows that you have followed the Action > Reflection > Input sequence. The part when you found that there was something you could not do is where you reflect (and perhaps think about previous machines you have had, possible reasons why you cannot engage the desired functionality, etc.) before taking some input by eventually reading the manual.

You may be the kind of person who wants to set time aside, when you can fully concentrate on installing the new coffee machine – having first given due thought to where you are going to physically place the unit, how you are going to connect it to your water supply and where you can conveniently locate all the consumables you need.

This kind of approach would mean that you are most likely a REFLECTION oriented person, and when you do settle down to install the unit you will probably consult the manual to make sure you are complying with any restrictions on where it can physically be placed (e.g. allowing room for ventilation, etc.) thus following the sequence Reflection > Input > Action (Action being when you actually power up the coffee machine and begin to try to use it).

Or you may just be the kind of person that opens the box and only takes out the manual to start with, leaving everything else where it is until you have had a good old read! That's you leading with INPUT, and then following the sequence Input > Action > Reflection – where the Action is you using the machine after having read the manual and the Reflection being when you are considering the results of your Actions and whether you have successfully mastered your new coffee machine, or whether you need to take further input from the manual.

In my experience, Geeks are more likely to be Action oriented, but in my Masterclasses there are invariably one or two people who prefer to read the manual first (Input led). There is nothing wrong with any of these approaches – it just comes down to the type of person you are. The main thrust here is that you consider that the audience's Learning Styles may be different from your own.

Remember three things to note about the Learning Cycle:

1. All three parts need to take place for learning to occur.
2. You will have a personal preference about where you like to start in the Cycle. This is an indication of your Learning Style.
3. If you are not careful, you will assume that your audience has the same Learning Style as you – and this is a big mistake!

Now that we have the basic theory established let's go through some examples of mini learning sessions leading with each of the three phases:

Input led session

E.g. How to write a program in the Python programming language.

INPUT: Trainer spends two hours on an introductory session, teaching people how to construct and run a program that will print 'Hello World' on the screen.

ACTION: Students have one hour to go through an exercise based on what the trainer has just covered.

REFLECTION: Trainer facilitates a session where the students compare experiences in getting this program running and compare the results they obtained.

Action led session
E.g. How to add an email account on a brand-new iPhone.

ACTION: Trainer gives each student a brand-new iPhone and tells them to add an email account to it, with no further instruction, and Students then have to get on with the task.

REFLECTION: Each student speaks in front of the rest of the class to explain how far they got with adding the email account.

INPUT: The students who fully completed the task talk to those that did not go through the steps needed to get to a successful result.

Reflection led session

E.g. Identifying essential presentation skills.

REFLECTION: Trainer leads a 'flip chart session' where he asks the people in the group to call out the names of those they consider to be great public speakers. The trainer then asks the same group, looking at the names they have come up with, to identify the particular speaking skills that they all have in common.

INPUT: The trainer reveals a pre-made list of essential presentation skills, and checks off those that class has already identified, explaining the significance of each. The trainer also highlights any that the class did not identify.

ACTION: The class is split into small groups where they take turns to make short presentations that allow them to practice a particular presentation skill from the list.

As each member of your audience will have their own preferred Learning Style, therefore falling into one of three groups, your job is to try to identify what those Learning Styles are and make sure that you cater for them within your presentation.

The next question is, of course: how do we find out what peoples' Learning Styles are?

You will recall that in Protocol 1: Purpose we identified the three parties that would be brought together in the 'Outcome agreement'. They were the Presenter (you), the Sponsor (the person that asked you to make the presentation) and the Audience, and the point was to talk to those other parties to make sure you agreed the aim and objectives of your presentation.

At that stage, hopefully, you were able to talk to a representative or two of the audience. If so, those same people would be the exact ones that you can ask about Learning Styles. I understand that it is not always possible to talk to audience members, or representatives of them, ahead of the presentation – so our next consideration is to take an educated guess based on the type of audience we are going to be presenting to. Here are some examples of audiences that, admittedly, do make some sweeping generalisations.

Tech Support people: Action oriented
Human Resources people: Reflection oriented
Financial Controllers: Input oriented

It may be that we don't even know which type(s) of people are going to be in our audience, so in that case we just have to make sure there is something for everyone – in other words, ensure that you have part of your session that is Input led, another part that is Action led and a part that is Reflection led.

Your audience will really appreciate that you went out of your way to do this, although they may not really understand why. You may get comments afterwards like, "Great session! I really enjoyed the part where you had us try that new product out, without actually telling us how to do the things you wanted us to achieve first." That will be coming from an Action-oriented person. Or, someone might say, "The part where we started by considering what makes a great User Experience was really helpful!", which would come from a Reflection-oriented person. You get the point, I'm sure.

And, of course, you may use this feedback, especially if you spot some trends, to improve the effectiveness of future iterations of given presentations by bending the way you deliver the content towards the dominant Learning Styles you have identified in previous audiences.

Chapter Six - Protocol 4: Practise

"Amateurs practise until they get it right. Professionals practise until they can't get it wrong!"

I know what you're thinking, "Why have a whole chapter on Practise?"

Before we get to that, let's deal with 'practice' versus 'practise' (American readers can disregard the following paragraph):

Practice with a 'c' is the way things are done (e.g. "This is our usual practice") whereas practise with an 's' is to rehearse (e.g. "I rehearsed my presentation, or I practised my presentation"). The former is a noun, and the latter is a verb.

Please remember that a presentation is your time to shine, and you never know who might be watching, or who might see your presentation at a later date if it is being recorded. Many a person has been better appreciated, more recognised, maybe gained a promotion, a pay raise or even a new job in a new company on the basis of delivering a good presentation – and the amazing thing is that they may not even have known it!

Practising your presentation is of critical importance. It is the key to removing the vast majority of your nerves about giving the presentation (not all of them, as some may simply come from the prospect of being in front of a group of people), to ensuring you give the best delivery you can, and to achieving maximum value for your audience (and Sponsor, if there is one).

So why, with so much at stake, do people not devote themselves to lots and lots of practise? Over the years I have heard many different excuses. Here are the most popular ones:

"I don't have the time to practise."

Listen, if the presentation is worth delivering, then it's worth delivering it badly... Until you can deliver it well! The point of practising is that the poor deliveries are done in the run up to the one(s) in front of your intended audience(s), which will be the one(s) you deliver well!

One of the very special rules around presentations is this:

It does not matter why, or how, or whose fault it is. If a presentation is in any way not quite right, it will be perceived by your audience as YOUR FAULT! Because, after all, you are the presenter.

Practise is one of the things that is entirely within your power to do, as much as you need to – so make sure you TAKE THE TIME to practise as much as you need. If you are employed, and your boss asks you to make a presentation, make sure you agree with him/her well ahead of time that you will have enough time not only to create the presentation, but also to practise it adequately.

"I do my best presentations when I wing it!"

Utter rubbish! Or, if you're American, utter garbage! However good (or usually bad) a presentation is when someone has failed to properly plan, prepare and practise, it goes without saying that the presentation could be dramatically improved by putting in the time to properly plan, prepare and practise it!

Remember the attorney from Protocol 3: Plan! It would be a horrible prospect to have someone representing you who decided to "wing it" on the day of the hearing. Just as you would expect an attorney to fully plan, you would also expect them to have extensively practised making the case for your innocence.

Everyone with an ounce of common sense knows that a presentation of any kind where one wants or needs to appear well-prepared and polished, must be practised.

"I wanted to keep my powder dry for the actual, real audience."

I suppose that this is somewhat of a fair aim. I would, however, contend that by investing time into practising your presentation, it will undoubtedly have higher impact and gain more engagement from the real audience.

One thing I (and many others I have spoken with) have found over the years, is that practising your presentation makes you realise the points you are not able to expound upon well; the illustrations you had planned that will fall flat when said aloud. You will be grateful you did not "keep [your] powder dry" but instead are able to go into your presentation with confidence, knowing that what you are delivering is of utmost quality and value, and will land well with your audience.

Having made the case for putting the time and effort into practising your presentation, let's talk about what great practising actually is, and what it is not.

Good practising is not…

It is not going through your Power Point (or Keynote or Prezi, or whatever) slides one by one, and in your head thinking about what you will say against each slide, in rough terms – although this is what the average person would consider adequate.

It is not undertaking some kind of run-through the night before your presentation. You are unlikely to retain very much from this kind of "practise" and it may just reinforce your nerves. Teachers often advise their students that if they don't know the material by the night before the exam, they never will. It is too late, and a last-minute dash, for most people, will only create confusion and make things worse. You are much better off ensuring you are well-rested for the actual presentation.

Also, leaving things until the last-minute gives rise to the very real possibility that the time you have in mind for that last minute "practise" may disappear before your eyes – as something may crop up that eats into some or all of your allotted rehearsal time.

Actually, your practise times should have the same priority in your calendar as the delivery to the intended audience itself.

The good practice of good practise

Good practising involves delivering your presentation well ahead of your targeted delivery date, as you would do it to the real audience - out loud (not in your head) - to people that will ideally understand your subject matter. If that's not possible, then out loud delivery to an audience of friends or family would be the next best thing. And if that is not possible, deliver your presentation to the mirror and/or record it (video or audio) on your mobile phone.

The reason that practising out loud is a must is that it will allow you to hear how your delivery sounds, both in terms of detecting the presence of 'ums' and 'errs', etc. and also how your speech flows. It will allow you to hear clunky phrases or things that just don't sound right, and you will have the opportunity to change things (and practise the new version) well before you get in front of your intended audience, ensuring your ideas are conveyed the way you desire for them to be. Further, by practising your presentation you will gain a good idea of how long the delivery takes – and this is especially important if your session is part of a multi-presentation event like a conference, where timing is critical!

In my opinion, your best results will be achieved when you practise the whole presentation at least three times! BUT there are certain parts of the presentation that it will pay you to practise even more! What do you think those are?
If you answered the beginning and the end, you are spot on!

As mentioned elsewhere in this book, the beginning and end of your presentation (or of a given session if you are running a half-day, day-long or even longer programme) are your PRIME TIME! Your audience is at their most attentive and receptive during the beginning and end of your presentation – so make use of that fact and invest your time in practising those parts even more than you spend going through the whole thing. The beginning of your presentation is also the time when you may feel most nervous or anxious because you are concerned about getting things off to a great start, so I am sure you can see the value of going through that part so many times that you can almost deliver it on 'auto pilot' – in other words, you can deliver it well, in spite of other things that are going on or other thoughts you are having at the time.

Maybe you can design some opening sentences that you can use in many of your presentations, so that whatever you are doing, you can get off to a great start. This approach will be especially relevant if you tend to speak on a similar subject area over a few different presentations.

Here is an example of the opening lines I might use for one of my presentations about why Nerds aren't heard, or how Geeks can Speak better:

"Hello there, it's a great pleasure to be with you! My name is David Duffett and having spent many years in the technical world, mainly telecoms, I have come to the sad conclusion that technical people are not achieving the levels of success they should, simply because they are not communicating as well as they could!

By a quick show of hands, have you ever noticed that the technical people that develop and support a given product or service were not paid (and often not recognised) at anywhere near the same level as the people that sell that product or service?

Is that fair? No!

Now I am not suggesting that the Salespeople should be paid less, as I believe they bring a very valuable set of skills to the table – but what I am saying is that the technical people, or Geeks, should be better paid, recognised and rewarded.

I think the secret to making that happen is for them to be better communicators – not just to their colleagues and their customers, but to the world!

You see, after both giving and watching hundreds, maybe even thousands, of technical presentations, training sessions and conference speeches, it seemed to me that, honestly, most Geeks don't do the best job of speaking in public... And, as it turned out, I was reasonably good at presenting.

Just like the winner of a race doesn't need to be ten minutes ahead of the others, they only need to be one second ahead, I began to find that audiences would warm to my presentations – simply because they were that little bit more polished than the rest they had seen at whatever technical event we were at.

I then began to understand that the main reason for the success I had enjoyed was something that I had, for many years, viewed as a weakness… I had always thought that I was not technical enough! Although my degree is in Electronics and Electrical Engineering and I have specialised in Telecoms, I would forever meet people that seemed to understand whatever technology we were working on way better than me, but at the same time, I also noticed that I seemed to be in a more senior, more recognised (and quite possibly better paid) position in the corporate structure than they were – and it didn't seem right given their excellent capabilities.

Eventually it came to me that it was my ability to communicate, to present in public, that had played a major part in my success – and maybe the reason that I didn't feel technical enough was because I had nurtured a slightly different set of skills. While I had not had the same level of drive to get deeper into the technology, I had really invested in being the best speaker and presenter I could be.

This meant that I was just a bit different to many of the people that were on the Engineering side of whatever business I happened to be working in.

This realisation, coupled with a belief that all the amazing technical people I have come across in my career could be helped to be better presenters and speakers (if they want to be) is what has brought me to the place I am today!

I want to help! To give back! I want to Let the Geek Speak! I think it's time Nerds were heard! And I want to help Propeller Heads propel ahead with their careers and with their lives!
Are you ready? Let's go...!"

The above is an introduction I can use for almost any "Let the Geek Speak" type presentation or training session I deliver, and the more I use it the easier it just rolls off the tongue and provides a smooth and professional start to whatever I am doing.

By the way, did you notice that almost immediately, at the beginning of the second paragraph, I introduced some audience participation with the "quick show of hands"? We'll look at this in more detail in the chapter on Protocol 5: Participation, but at this stage – while we're considering the art of practising – please note the sooner you can get some interaction going with your audience, the faster you will engage them to come on a journey with you rather than making them feel that they are just a bunch of people that you are speaking at!

I don't want to be overly prescriptive on how you do the practising of your presentation, so please take the following as one way of doing things, or as some friendly suggestions that are given with your best interests at heart.

Assuming you have been through Protocols 1 to 3 (Purpose, Plan and Preferences) you should have the bones of a great presentation to practise – and I suggest the following:

1. Deliver your presentation out loud a couple of times all the way through by yourself.

Recording will probably be helpful, especially if you have times (like a car journey) when you can listen back to it with a degree of concentration. At this stage, don't worry at all if you lose your train of thought, or get stuck for words or whatever. Just force yourself to make your way through the whole thing. Feel free to use a script, or prompt cards, or whatever works best for you to help you with the verbal delivery.

Doing this will give you a good idea of the duration of your presentation, so you can tell whether you need to cut things out or expand anything in order to properly fit the time slot you have been allocated.

Just a quick note on the duration of your presentation: nobody has ever been annoyed or frustrated by a presentation being a little shorter than anticipated (by this, I do not mean embarrassingly short!). However, many, many people have been disheartened, disappointed or downright distraught, to say the least, by presentations that have gone on for too long. Never let your presentation go over its given time!

2. Give special attention to the beginning and ending of your presentation.

Consider how they might be made stronger, in terms of the impact you generate, by the language you use, and any fascinating facts, stories or questions which could instantly engage the audience. When practising aloud, you might realise you have not included impactful language or an exciting fact, and perhaps it would be beneficial to involve some form of audience participation or humour, to draw in the crowd from the outset. Be sure to focus on these two crucial areas by practising those parts individually several times more than the whole thing, until you feel happy with them.

3. Once you have gone through your entire presentation two or three times (enough to feel a bit more comfortable with it), you can progress to an 'Alpha' trial – in other words, delivering it to an 'internal' audience of colleagues, friends or family members.

Positive colleagues are great, as they can give feedback on your content as well as your style. Family and friends are also a very useful trial audience, as – not knowing the content – they can ask the 'dumb' questions that your colleagues may take for granted.

4. If you have the luxury of knowing some of your intended audience members and/or you can get some time with the 'Sponsor' of your talk, then you can do some 'Beta' trialling too!

The wonderful thing about practising your presentation is that you are getting familiar with the content of it, and this will allow you to progress to thinking not just about the content, but also about the style of your delivery – your pace, your pauses, your pitch, your pronunciation and lots of other aspects. Although the content might be fantastic, if it is not delivered in a suitable, engaging style, it will not be received as it should be. Remember – if it's easy to deliver, it will be easy to receive!

Delivering a presentation is somewhat like driving a car. If you can drive, you will remember that during your early driving lessons, the car would swerve a little while you changed gear or turned on the indicator. That is because you were taking your mind off the steering of the vehicle while you were thinking of those other things. However, the more you practised your driving, the better you got at steering the vehicle while also doing other things like changing gear – because driving was becoming easier for you, and ultimately it became second nature. Now, you don't even have to think about steering while you undertake a range of other operations like turning on the indicator, changing gears, checking your mirrors, etc. So it is with your presentations. The more you practise, the more comfortable you get with delivering a given presentation, while at the same time monitoring your own delivery. You will then be able to gauge from your own self-listening (as well as "reading" your audience – more about that in Chapter 10: The Exponential Booster) how well you are doing in terms of the speed of your delivery, whether you are losing people with the technicalities you are using, if your audience needs a break, etc. Therefore, you can manage yourself as a speaker – but all of this only comes with PRACTISE!

To miss practising your presentation is to miss an open goal in terms of an easy way to improve the structure, content and delivery of your presentation.

Practise really is the low-hanging fruit of presentational goodness. If you prioritise practise, you will undoubtedly reap the associated rewards: the recognition that a well-practised and polished presentation often garners from an appreciative audience!

Chapter Seven - Protocol 5: Participation

Nothing engages an audience like participation. I have never forgotten this invaluable equation a friend once shared with me:

INVOLVEMENT = COMMITMENT

If you involve your audience in your presentation, their commitment to the outcomes you have agreed with them (see Protocol 1: Purpose) will significantly increase. There is a saying, sometimes attributed to Benjamin Franklin, sometimes identified as a Chinese Proverb, that goes something like this:

"Tell me and I will forget, show me and I might remember, but INVOLVE me and I will UNDERSTAND!"

So, as you can see, there are two great reasons to get your audience involved in your presentation: (1) they will be more committed to the agreed outcomes and, (2) they will better understand the message you are conveying and the information you wish them to retain.

As human beings, we like to be involved in things to learn. We don't often want things done to us but seem to prefer having things done with us - and presentations are very much like this. An audience will remain unengaged and uninvolved unless and until you, the Presenter, open the door of participation.

Once that door of participation has been opened, the audience are in on the journey and you, the Presenter, become the Guide!

One of the fundamental things about the human condition is that we tend to be suspicious about the things that other people tell us, especially when those other people are at the front of a room trying to 'sell' something – whether that is a product, a service or even an idea (though there is nothing wrong with some healthy scepticism). However, if someone just like us tells us something, we're more prone to believe it – and if we tell ourselves something, then it is an undeniable truth.

So, how do you encourage the audience to tell themselves such truths? There are several means to convey truth to people in a way that they will personally relish and understand.

Stories

Stories are a very powerful tool in this way. You see, when you tell a relevant story to people that contains a lesson, the hearers of the story draw their own conclusions, even if it is a conclusion that you have engineered to be drawn. In other words – they tell themselves – and because they told themselves, then it must be the truth!

I heard a very neat and touching example of this in Church one Sunday. The Preacher was talking about people being annoyed that it costs money to run a Church, and he made the point that a living, vibrant Church does cost money!

He went on to tell a true story about an American man, whom we'll call Tim, who had been grumbling about his Church asking for money to cover running costs etc. One of Tim's friends, Michael, told Tim how God had blessed him and his wife with a son some years ago, and how that son had cost money from the day he was born. First, there was the hospital bill, then nappies (diapers), clothes, food, decorating the nursery, toys, etc... the list went on. As the boy grew up, the bills got bigger! School equipment, books, more clothes, holidays, hobbies, driving lessons, a car, and so on. Then the boy went to College and the bills got even bigger. Michael explained that while his son was a Senior at College, he had very tragically passed away from an unforeseen health condition.
Tim quickly burst out, "I am so sorry to hear that. It must have been terrible for you and your wife."

Michael responded to his grumbling friend, "Yes, it was devastating – but you know what? He hasn't cost us a penny since."

Tim was lost for words as he understood the simple, but powerful lesson. When something or someone is living and growing, there are costs to meet, and that we should be glad to meet those costs as they arise.

As you can see, relevant stories are a great thing to build into a presentation – because during the story your audience will tell themselves things that are much more powerful (to them) than anything you could have said directly.

Choose your stories well though. Make sure they are about your audience and solving their problems, not about you.

There are lots of resources around to help with the art of storytelling and I can recommend StoryQuadrant by Jon Billett, available at storyquadrant.com

Questions Are The Answer

Questions are also of vital importance in presentations – both questions from the audience to you, the Presenter, and more importantly, questions from you to the audience.

The fact of the matter is that all (properly addressed) questions are always answered! Let me reiterate that:

ALL (PROPERLY ADDRESSED) QUESTIONS ARE ALWAYS ANSWERED!

Please let me explain…

Whenever we are asked a question, we can't help but answer it – whether we actually verbalise the answer or not. Let's try it out:

What was the name of your first pet?

I would be very surprised if you have not already answered that question in your mind (you may have even spoken the name out loud) or concluded that you have never had a pet. So, what do I mean by a PROPERLY ADDRESSED question? What I mean is a question that your audience really feels is addressed to them.

How do we ensure that your audience feels you are really talking to them? We achieve that by endeavouring to establish and maintain effective eye contact during the presentation, especially when we are asking questions. Then, when you ask a question, your audience will ALL answer that question in their own minds – even though they will probably not verbalise that answer.

There is an old technique that encapsulates what to do pretty well. It's called "Pose, Pause, Pounce" and it assumes that you have a good connection (or good rapport) with your audience and that you have been engaging them in effective eye contact as you lead up to the question.

First, you POSE the question. You ask your audience the question.

Next, you PAUSE. This gives them all the opportunity to answer the question in their minds – because you asked the question while you were talking to them.

Last, you POUNCE (in a friendly way) on one particular member of the audience to give an answer to the question out loud – and then you give feedback on that answer.

This allows the whole audience to evaluate the answer they came up with in their minds. Were they correct or not? Can they see why the answer that you, the Presenter, gave (by confirming the validity of the answer of the person you "pounced" on, or by correcting it) is best? You may also give a little prize to the person you selected – whether they got the correct answer or not – for their participation.

Please understand that the above is just one technique, and while very useful, should not be overplayed to the point of monotony. Questions are massively important in all parts of life, and your presentations will be better for the inclusion of relevant questions to, and from, your audience. There is a great book about the power of questions – 'Questions Are The Answer' by Alan Pease. Check it out if you want to delve deeper into the art of questions.

We need to consider the types of questions that there are. Generally, we can split questions into two categories:

(1) Open questions (sometimes known as 'fishing' questions). These generally start with What, When, Where, Who, Why or How – and the answer could be anything! We use this type of question when we are trying to explore a topic or establish someone's understanding of a given subject, etc.

Example open questions: How do you feel about your age? What is your understanding of the purpose of the monarchy in the UK? What would you do if you were the Supervisor of this group?

(2) Closed questions (sometimes known as 'shooting' questions). These have a definite answer, which

is probably ‘yes’, ‘no’ or a specific piece of information.

Example closed questions: How old are you? Have you passed your driving test? Do you understand how water turns into ice?

Notes on questions

Always make it easy, fun and rewarding for people to answer questions. If you ask a question and an audience member is good enough to answer, and then you belittle them, actively disagree with them, or take issue with them in some other way, how likely is it that anyone else will want to answer a question thereafter?

If you have been explaining a new concept to a group of people, which question is more likely to receive an honest response?

(a) Does everyone understand that?
(b) How are folk feeling about this new information?

I would argue (b) is better as it allows people to explain how they are feeling (even if they explain that they are finding the new concept tough to grasp), rather than admitting they don’t understand.
Mix up the types of questions you ask, and make sure you draw answers from all over the room.

Encourage questions from your audience where possible. Honour those who ask a question, even if it is a question that you don't like!

If the audience is not forthcoming, ask yourself a question by saying something like "At this point in the presentation, some people are probably asking themselves, how am I going to find time to learn this new technique?" and then you can answer the question, "Well, would you believe that with just 10 minutes per day for two weeks, you can be totally proficient!"

Show of Hands

Having the audience do a quick show of hands is a great way to allow everyone to see the answer visually. This is especially effective when trying to highlight various experiences or opinions. For example, if you said, "I am here today to speak about road safety. By a show of hands, how many people here have ever been in a traffic accident of some kind?" It is always a good idea to raise your hand as you come to the end of the sentence to show the audience how to indicate their answer. Immediately the audience will see (probably confirming what they already know) that involvement in an accident is a pretty common experience.

The above is an example of a 'shooting' question (that only has a 'yes' or 'no' answer) and these are really the only type that a show of hands is good for. You couldn't really ask a question like, "How have you been affected by a road traffic accident?" and get an answer by a show of hands. Do you see my point?

A great use of the show of hands is when you are trying to encourage a change in behaviour, or you are in a sales situation, and you want your audience to know that a good number of people have already made that change or made that purchase. You can ask them to signal that with a show of hands.

Let's say the point of your talk is to encourage the adoption of a new working practice and you happen to know that a reasonable proportion of people in your audience are already using this new working practice and finding it beneficial.

This would allow you, probably reasonably early on in the presentation, to say something like, "Before I go into the top-level details of the new practise, how many here have already adopted this new way of doing things?"

If 70% of the people enthusiastically raise their hands, the remaining 30% will look like they are lagging behind, and it will be easier to 'sell' them on adopting that new practice. Assuming that you have good rapport with your audience, a good follow-up to that show of hands would be to walk towards one of the folk who raised their hands (or point to them if you cannot walk towards them) and say something like, "And what differences have you noticed now that you have adopted this new working practice?"

When that audience member outlines one of two of the benefits they are now seeing, this is like pure gold for helping those who have not yet made the change to do so – because it is not you telling them to do something, it is one of their own (a fellow audience member) and so therefore is much more powerful.

Sharing Experiences

Another great means of participation is asking people in your audience to share their experiences in a way that will help other audience members get the point or understand the challenge, or whatever it is that you are trying to achieve. Let's take a scenario where you are briefing a group on a new product (it could be software or hardware) and your main aim is to help the group learn the main features and benefits of this new product. You may well have thought things through and created a great presentation with some appropriate slides to show the main points etc. but your session will take on an extra dimension of validity if you ask your audience who has actually used or tested the new product.

When a few hands go up, because that is the response you have encouraged, you can ask one of those people to share their experiences (good or bad) with the group. If they share a bad experience, this may be a teaching opportunity because they were somehow using it incorrectly or did not understand how to use it. It may be that there is a problem with the new product that needs to be addressed, and you have created the right situation to identify that issue, and you can feed it back to the product team. Equally, your handy audience member may highlight a great advantage or something they really like about the new product – and you can work with what they have mentioned and tie it into one of the key points you want to reinforce, or – even better – get another audience member to make the link for you!

E.g. "Steve says that while he was testing the new product, he found the user interface much easier to work with than the previous version. Looking at the key benefits on this slide (assuming you have the key benefits slide up at that point), which one do you think the 'easier user interface' relates to?"

Tami immediately answers, "Faster results", because she can see that if the user interface is easier to work with, users will achieve what they need to more quickly.

Audience members with relevant experience can be a real asset to your presentation! Show them your appreciation!

Group Exercises

Another great way to engage your audience and break things up a bit is to get them involved in a group exercise. You may wish to have them move around in the room to form groups, which can act to refresh their energy levels, or you may set up the room 'café style' (using round tables) so that those around each table form into a group for given exercises.

The type and length of any exercise is for you to choose, and it could range from a brief discussion about the key learning points of the session (which is always a very worthwhile exercise, as people inevitably pick things up from their classmates that they missed themselves) to a structured preparation for a further exercise.

Here is an example. When I personally teach geeks to speak in my live training, one of the things I like to do is have small groups discuss the advantages and disadvantages of the various types of visual aids that can be used in a given presentation. So, I might have group A discuss and agree the top 5 advantages of using something like PowerPoint and a Projector, and also come up with the top 5 disadvantages of using a flip chart. I will have group B do exactly the opposite (disadvantages of PowerPoint with Projector and advantages of the flip chart).

I will then orchestrate a good-natured and friendly 'battle' between the two groups – to compare their answers to see which comes out on top. Of course, I may have had a previous exercise where I had the individual groups brainstorm between themselves to see how many 'visual aids' for a presentation they could come up with between them!

The list of useful exercises you can build into a presentation is only limited by your imagination. The key is to ensure that any exercises you use really are valuable, and that you have taken into account the preferences of your audience (see Protocol 3: Preferences) when evaluating which to go with.

Fill in the Gaps

If there is certain information that you want or need your audience to leave your presentation with, you may have prepared a hand-out for them to follow along with or just take away at the end of your session. These can be turned into great participation tools by leaving words (or even simple pictures) out, and having your audience fill in those gaps as you go through your presentation. This is based upon the principle of incompletion – that people just do not like incomplete things.

There is something about a _ _ _ _ _ space that make us want to fill it, and you can take advantage of that desire to gain useful participation and learning –remember, "Involve me and I will _ _ _ _ _ _ _ _ _ _ _!"

Do you see what I did there?

As you probably guessed, the _ _ _ _ _ _ _ _ words (I can't stop myself) were 'blank' and 'understand', and then 'correct'.

The above is a very short list of just a few ways of encouraging participation in your presentations – and you will see, hear and feel the rewards of being deliberate about the modes of participation you use as a Presenter as you put them into practice in your future sessions.

Of course, there are many, many more ways of having your audience join in – and we explore further options in the live events. See geekspeakhq.com for upcoming dates.

What about over/unwanted participation?

"I spent the first half of the presentation trying to coax Ron out of his shell - and the second half trying to put him back in it! Boy, that man can talk!"

It's possible, perhaps even probable, that you will at some stage experience 'over/unwanted participation' of some kind during a presentation you are leading. It could be an audience member who always answers every question out loud, not allowing others to get in with their answers.

Maybe they over contribute with stories or experiences, or perhaps they are just wanting to show the other members of the audience that they know more about the given subject than you do! This is where your audience or 'classroom' management skills will be required. You will perfect these over time, but in any event, I want to share a few ways of dealing with this kind of occurrence in order to help your presentations go more smoothly.

The first thing to realise is that if there are people in your audience who know more about the subject at hand, then welcome them – don't fear them. Once you come to understand that an audience member has more knowledge and/or experience than you do, turn them into a friendly resource (getting them on your side, rather than possibly being against you) by acknowledging their expertise, and asking their permission to come back to them for a contribution or two during your presentation. You can do that with something like this response to one of their early contributions: "Thank you, Jim! It seems like you've done a lot with this new product already. Would it be OK to come back to you to share some of your experience towards the end of the presentation?" In one sentence you have thanked them for their previous contribution, acknowledged their standing, and (probably) shut them down until you are ready to hear from them again later!

If someone insists on continuing their contributions to the detriment of the participation of others, you can deal with it without getting personal by asking for some contributions from another part of the room. For example, if they are in the front part of the audience, you can say, "We've heard a bit from this front part of the room, I'm interested to hear from the back part. Who back there would care to comment?"

For extreme cases of unwanted participation, it is better to let fellow audience members deal with the situation, rather than personally reprimanding someone in front of the audience (which may contain the unwanted contributor's friends or co-workers). You might say something like, "Bob has just told us about his recent experiences. What do other people think?" This opens the door for another audience member to explain that they have heard enough from Bob, or that his stories are not relevant, or that he should quieten down and allow others to contribute. Thus, Bob is given the message, but not by you!

There are a few 'quick fixes' we can deploy to aid positive participation. Here are a couple:

If someone has their arms folded – hand something (where possible, relevant to your presentation) to them. It causes them to unfold their arms and gives them something to look at.

If you know someone has relevant knowledge or experience and likes to share, acknowledge this early in your presentation, and let them know you will be asking them to contribute at some stage. This means you are less likely to get untimely or unwanted input from them.

Participation is the key to potentially massive engagement, so it's worth devoting time to specifically consider what means and modes of getting people involved you would like to deploy.

Pro tip: When presenting in other countries or cultures, be sure to check up with someone that knows concerning what is likely to be acceptable/effective participation for your audience.

Chapter Eight - Protocol 6: Performance

Finally, we reach the Performance protocol! This is the part where you actually deliver the presentation that you have been working on across the first five protocols.

Nerves

The first subject I would like to address in this Protocol is nerves. Most people do have some kind of nervous feeling when speaking in front of an audience, at least for the first few minutes. Perhaps with practice and experience, these nerves start to disappear later in your presentation, but I believe that this is still a worthwhile subject for discussion. Now, if you have gone through the five preceding protocols – Purpose, Plan, Preferences, Practise (this is a big one; a key reason some people are nervous is that they never actually practise!), and Participation, I would submit that you will have eradicated 90% of those nerves – simply by following those first five protocols! This is because you will know what to say, how to say it, and how to introduce the presentation properly. You will feel comfortable because you've practised, and will involve participation (because remember, friendly interaction really engages your audience and puts them at ease). Although we can get rid of most nerves by preparing using the suggested protocol framework, it is inevitable that there will still be some remaining – so let's talk about how to deal with those.

I would like to make it clear that there is nothing wrong with feeling a little bit nervous; in fact, it is a good sign. Being nervous shows that you care about the subject at hand and your audience, and that you want to give it your best shot – it is important to you – so it is completely natural to have nerves.

However, there are ways that nerves can adversely affect the presenter. If someone feels nervous, they may lack focus, and their mind might begin to jump around. Some people struggle with shortness of breath, which could inhibit necessary vocal projection. A common problem with nerves is that they cause many people to speed up their vocal delivery when giving a presentation, which will not communicate well to the audience, in terms of the comfort level of the presenter with being in front of them and / or the contents of the presentation itself.

There are studies to show that giving a fast delivery may not necessarily affect the audience's ability to take in information; however, fast delivery does psychologically communicate to the audience that you don't want to be there because you're racing through the material, and this will be picked up by them, even if only subconsciously. This is something we want to avoid where possible.

So, what are nerves and why do we have them?

Nerves are your body's natural response to a perceived or imagined threat, and in turn, some people deem nerves to be a result of fear. Whilst there is no physical threat to fear in giving a presentation, our perceived threat is largely to do with fear of the audience's response and the outcomes of a presentation. As presenters, a great way for us to remember "fear" is the following:

False
Evidence
Appearing
Real

In other words, too often we are made nervous by prospects that are entirely unlikely. With this in mind, some good questions to ask yourself are:

What is the best thing that could happen when you deliver your presentation?
The best-case scenario is that you walk out on stage confidently, and the audience stand and applaud you before you've even delivered any material because they know they're in for a treat. You begin the presentation and your opening is excellent. You engage the audience naturally. You ask questions and there's full interaction, the audience smile, and are very receptive. They are

smiling and nodding as you give your three key points, and you can see them taking it all in – they love it! You get to the end, you solicit any questions there might be before the summary and receive very sensible questions which clearly show they have been taking in all that you're saying and liking it; they've warmed to you as a person. You summarise and use a powerful triple ending – the use of three sentences that all start with or use the same word or phrase (e.g. "It's been a pleasure speaking with you this evening. It's been a pleasure showing you how to achieve more with your presentations. But the real pleasure will come for you when you implement these protocols and thus receive all the rewards that come from being a Nerd that gets heard! Thank you!). There's an immediate standing ovation, and the audience clap heartily until you leave the stage. If you're selling a product or service, they come to you afterwards to let you know they want to buy it and perhaps agree to a business deal with you there and then.

What is the worst thing that could happen?

Alternatively, the worst-case scenario: as you're walking out on stage, you trip over awkwardly, then stumble about and make a fool of yourself as you try to get up. You're red and embarrassed, and your clothing is a bit dislodged – people can tell you're very uneasy. You stutter out your first few words, and you can see the audience really losing any empathy they did have, because they can see you're just totally unprepared. You mumble and splutter, your delivery is extremely poor. It's torturous going through the presentation, it really feels awful and you can't wait to get it over with. When you finish, no questions are forthcoming, but at least you remember to make a summary. However, it doesn't really work out, so the audience gives a charitable round of applause but you can tell their hearts aren't in it. Nobody comes and speaks to you afterwards. You walk back from the stage with your head hung low, knowing that you've done a terrible job.

What is likely to happen?

What's likely to happen is that you come out on stage, and you've put together a great presentation which has purpose (aims agreed), is planned (structured well), considers the audience's preferences (you've thought about their learning styles), you've practised (you know the flow, and your material, very well), and you've factored in participation (to draw your audience in). Are you going to be perfect? Probably not! But are the audience willing you to do well? They probably are! The presentation that is easy to deliver is easy to receive. If you feel at ease delivering your presentation, the audience are going to feel at ease receiving it. Near the end, there might be one or two questions, and then you finish with your summary, a bang ending, and people give a kind round of applause.

The more you present, the better you will be able to read the audience in terms of their engagement and satisfaction (or even delight) with what you're doing.

When you analyse things in this way, you do realise that fear really is False Evidence Appearing Real.

Perhaps it's not going to be amazing, but it's definitely going to be acceptable. And remember that the more you do this, the better you will get at it! Again, I'm not talking about having a quick flick through your slides and thinking about what you're going to say but rather practising all of this out loud to a real-life audience. The more you practise, the better your chance of delivering a spot-on presentation.

If you have had past successes, think about those times and consider the things that made them go well. Consider what you associate with those successes. Perhaps you were wearing a particular jacket, or blouse, and remember succeeding at those times. Not that these items give any special power, but you might associate them with doing well at something and may want to incorporate them into future presentations.

If you still feel nerves are an issue, practise, practise, practise, and if you continue to feel that way, then hop onto geekspeakhq.com and head to the Book Resources section, where you will find further useful tools, such as

"10 ways to reduce nerves when delivering a presentation".

Although nerves will certainly play a part, and we may not hit every single goal first time, let's always aim to make the presentation an amazing experience for our audience.

Vocal Delivery

Another issue to address is vocal delivery. There are many aspects to a powerful vocal performance, namely:

Projection: this is the volume and resonance of your voice, so that even the people at the back can hear. Does the venue have good acoustics, or will you need a microphone and speaker system? Sometimes it's overkill in a smaller space, but other times it's entirely necessary.

Pitch: high pitch tends to convey excitement, perhaps frenzy and nerves, but a low pitch is very reassuring, and can help people understand why what you're saying is of critical importance.

Pace: if you speed up, this builds excitement; but a slower pace will enable you to put across more serious points, and your audience will feel and understand this.

Pauses: these are very, very important especially when you're asking questions. For example, if you're maintaining eye contact with your audience (one-on-one if they're a smaller audience, or if a larger audience and that's physically impossible, making eye contact with sections so they all feel like they're being addressed), a pause is going to be extremely effective. If you asked, "How do cats impact road safety?" and then left a pause, people would have the opportunity to answer that question in their mind and, as stated above, what people tell themselves is so much more important than what you tell them.

Power: though the power of your voice is related to the projection aspect, power, in this case, is more indicative of the amount you've practised and prepared your presentation. If you have not practised out loud to a real audience, particularly the first few minutes of your presentation, it is not likely you are going to begin the presentation with power and confidence in your voice. This is also related to how well you know the material as this will be conveyed in the strength and power that your voice brings forth.

What happens if you don't change the pitch or pace? Or include pauses? Well, if you don't change the pitch, your voice will be monotonous – and you don't really want your audience thinking or feeling that they're in the middle of a presentation that's monotonous (i.e. boring).

Of course, the words you say are just one part of face-to-face communication. The way you say these words can have a massive impact on their perceived meaning! So it really is important to learn to use your voice effectively when delivering a presentation. Also important is non-verbal communication (body language, movement, gaze, posture, facial expressions).

Another thing to think about is verbal tics and habits. Are there things that you're always saying, like, "know what I mean", "see what I mean" or "mmm"? If you say these more than you need to, your audience is going to pick up on this and it will be a distraction. Many people repeatedly use words like "basically" when giving presentations, which is off-putting for an audience and should be avoided. This is because it is patronising; you're effectively saying "I'm going to break this down for you and make it more basic, because you're a bit simpler than I am". By indicating that you're more intelligent than them, you are not going to win the favour of your audience, so try to be aware of words you might continually throw in which would be a distraction during your delivery. Verbal fillers do not add any value, further – they also distract and detract from your content. Equally, are there motions you frequently make that viewers would pick up on? Do you throw your arms in a certain way, gesture with your hands repeatedly in the same fashion, or fiddle with your pen? All these things have to pass the "Is It A Distraction?" test, and should be considered prior to your performance.

As mentioned above, body language is incredibly important when delivering a presentation. People are more likely to take in with their eyes than their ears. A presenter's posture can give away a lot about how they are feeling. Are they stood tall and erect, shoulders back with head held high, or are they slouched, shoulders slumped, looking at floor and not the audience? The former conveys confidence and comfort, whereas the latter presents insecurity and lack of enthusiasm. As well as giving an unfavourable impression to the audience, poor posture can also affect your voice and limit projection. All these things should be taken into consideration when preparing to perform.

If you're trying to convey an enthusiastic message, what happens if your body language is not congruent? The power of your message is lost. Whether you move around the stage too much or stay behind the podium the entire time - all of these things can have a negative effect on your presentation.

Personal Impact

Personal impact plays a vital role in the effectiveness of your performance. When you show up to give a presentation, what impression are you giving? Do you turn up looking like you're excited to be there? Are you enthusiastic about the matter of which you have come to speak? As presenters, we absolutely must show enthusiasm. We can remember this using the last four letters of the word, "IASM", standing for "I am sold myself". It is no good giving a presentation about something you're not personally interested in and excited about. If you've been asked to give a presentation at work, and you're genuinely not interested in the subject matter at all, perhaps reconsider giving the presentation and perhaps suggest that there might be someone better for this particular task. This is acceptable, because to excel, it is imperative that you actually care about what you're presenting. For example, this would be the case for me if I were asked to do a health and safety talk at work. I understand that it is important, crucial, in fact, but sadly this doesn't float my boat, and so I am not going to have a huge amount of personal impact or introduce the behaviour changes desired because I can't muster the enthusiasm for it myself.

The way you dress can also have a big impact on your message. It can affect your rapport significantly. Imagine with me that you're in a plumber's merchant, where real plumbers go to buy radiators, shower units, copper pipes, waste pipes etc., when a guy walks in that wants to get a great deal on a piece of hardware. If he walked in a three-piece suit with smart shoes, cufflinks, cutaway collar, a nice tie, clean shaven and smelling nice, and said "I say, my good man, what are the best prices you can give me on this thermostatic radiator valve?" Well, I would say his chances are zero, because he's instantly broken rapport before he even had a chance to create it since he's shown up not looking the part. Say instead that he first took off his jacket, rolled up his sleeves, unbuttoned his top button before entering the place, then looked around at the hardware, and had a small conversation with the Assistant beginning with, "Alright mate...", prior to enquiring about the best deal. He is much more likely to succeed.

If you are dressed incongruently with your message and delivery, it's going to have a negative effect. You don't want to be too hot – it's never good to be profusely sweating whilst giving the presentation - but equally you don't want to be so cold that it's distracting you from being able to present as you ought to. If you're going to be filmed, be careful of colours and patterns because they might not show up well on screen or on a video recording. Go for loose fitting clothes and avoid anything too tight since this will not contribute positively to your physical comfort nor your professional appearance. If you are going to be on screen, avoid busy patterns that cause issues on camera.

Language and volume also play a vital role in personal impact. For example, using colloquial or shouting words for comedic effect. I am not talking about being nasty or aggressive, but instead simply using a louder volume at times to help engage and perhaps humour your audience. I remember being particularly gratified after a course I had taught a few years back in this respect. I had shouted a certain key word all week, for comedic value and to get it into peoples' memories, and by the second or third day other class members were shouting it when asking questions or helping one another. From this I knew good rapport had been established and I was pleased that they were cottoning on so well not only to the material, but to the class ambience.

What is your thing?

Your "thing" is a way that your audience can remember you. This could take many different forms, for example, wearing a hat. Perhaps every time you give a presentation you wear a hat, the same hat, or different hats. Maybe one day you show up in a trilby, and the next day you come in a fedora, and the last day you come in a top hat. People are going to recognise that's your thing - you're the person with the hat! Another 'thing' could be giveaways...

For a long part of my career giving presentations in diverse places such as the USA, Singapore, Malaysia, Indonesia and other Asian countries, Latin America (countries like Brazil, Chile, Colombia, Mexico etc.), one thing I would always do as a British person is take some Cadbury chocolate. Over time I developed a reputation as the "candy man" in America. If they asked questions, or answered them, I would give them a chocolate, and it put me in people's memories.

I knew a guy that would always wear Hawaiian shirts to give presentations, and another who always wore tie-dye shirts. When we were at conferences, they were always very easy to spot!

Maybe your thing is a certain style of delivery. Maybe it's comedic deadpan. I saw an excellent presentation once from a Facilities Manager who was in one of my classes. I had advised him to try and start off with an engaging question, but not necessarily to copy someone else's style. Opening his presentation, he simply leant back on the desk (at the front of the room), folded his arms, and said, "Right, how many people would like the afternoon off...?", and, of course, everyone put their hands up. Then, he said, "...In hospital?. Because that's where you're going to end up if you don't listen to my short presentation on health and safety in the workplace". It was extremely funny, and people warmed to it immediately. It was a straightforward dead pan delivery and there wasn't anything extremely charismatic about it, but there was a certain humour that people really appreciated.

Think about what your "thing" might be... It could be that you give away fruit when people answer questions correctly. It might be a catch phrase that you use repeatedly. When working for Digium and teaching Asterisk, the open-source telephony software, I developed a phrase: "It's beautiful, and it's free!". Soon people were saying it back to me and I knew that I had left an impression in people's minds.

The most important thing about your thing, is that it really is your thing!
Something that you feel comfortable about being identified with and remembered for.
With the ending of your presentation being so important, it is worth spending time on crafting a real BANG QS3 ending (as opposed to letting your presentation whimper out!). Revisit Protocol 2: Plan, where endings are covered in more detail, if you like.

Chapter Nine -
Protocol 7: Post-Event

So much power and potential are lost when a presentation is not followed up properly, and this is exactly why the Post-Event protocol is an important part of the 7 Power Presenting Protocols contained in this book.

You will remember, in Protocol 1: Purpose, we began with the end in mind (to borrow from Stephen Covey's '7 Habits of Highly Effective People') when we agreed the desired outcomes of our presentation with both the audience and the sponsor.

Further, we agreed those outcomes at two levels – the specific focus of the presentation itself AND the desired outcomes at the wider business level. Also, we agreed when we would check to see that these outcomes had been achieved.

What this means is that we have precisely the framework and information we need to ensure that our presentation is followed up with a professional and predictable process that gets the best outcomes for your audience, your sponsor and YOU yourself!

To use the simple example found elsewhere in this book, you have agreed the following desired outcomes with your sponsor and your audience when you were working on Protocol 1: Purpose:

1) Presentation outcome:
To familiarise the audience with the five most important features of version 3.0 of product X.

2) Business outcome:
To reduce the volume of technical support calls for Product X by 25% following the introduction of version 3.0.
You will see that measurement of the outcomes is very easy, because we defined them so specifically in the first place.

At the end of the presentation, we can use a suitable method (maybe a quiz or the participants giving a practical demonstration) to establish whether our purpose/desired outcome has been achieved.

If we find out that people are not able to demonstrate the level of familiarity required, we may deduce that a further presentation, or delivery of the information in a different way is needed.

Then, when people have had a chance to put their learning into action back in their jobs, at the agreed time (let's say a month after the presentation), we can check with the Sponsor whether the business-level outcome, in this example the reduction in volume by 25% of the tech support calls, has been achieved.

The above are the visible and, arguably, most important parts of the Post-Event protocol. They help to measure the success of your session, but they are really the 'tip of the iceberg' in terms of the variety of things we can do both to ensure that the presentation we made has the maximum effect AND to build the relationship with our clients (whether internal like our boss and colleagues, or external like conference organisers or others that might buy our services).

Seek Feedback

Gathering feedback about what the participants thought of your session is good practice and will help you optimise future iterations of this presentation.

It can be done via a paper-based 'happy sheet' at the end of the session, although using an online form accessed via a QR-code is much more usual these days. The latter has the advantage of being easier logistically (no need to print the forms out, and then distribute, gather and go through them manually or scan them) and the data collected can easily, and often automatically, end up in a spreadsheet for analysis.

Whatever kind of end-of-the-session feedback you would like to collect, you will get more responses if you have participants do it while they are still with you.

Sending an email or text/WhatsApp message after the session may get some responses, but the percentage will be considerably lower than the 100% you can get while people are in the room with you.

You can even collect feedback via the QR-code link to a form method before you finish, then summarise your main points!

Having said all that, it will still be very advantageous to make contact with a selection of participants personally via a brief phone call at a given period after the session (e.g. one week) in order to garner further feedback now that they have had a chance to reflect on the session and put the information you gave them to use.

Personal Follow Ups

Sending an email after the event to all participants gives you the opportunity to show that you are grateful for their time and their engagement during your session.

It also provides an easy mechanism (clicking reply) for them to get in touch with you if they would like to.

You can supply a PDF of your slides, a recording of the session (if one was made), or any additional resources you may have promised or referenced during your talk.

And, if there were any questions that you couldn't or didn't answer during your session, this same email or a second one at a later date will allow you to provide those answers.
Further content for a follow up email can include a summary of your main points, and if there were any polls conducted, the actual results obtained (and possibly some analysis or conclusions).

Human to Human Relationships

Be sure to get 'LinkedIn' with the participants in your session. It's good practice to invite people to connect with you during your presentation (e.g. via a QR-code or some other method), but you can be proactive with those that did not take up your offer, especially those that you noticed were more engaged or showed a particular interest in something you shared.

Feel free to start conversations about your content or related topics with individuals or relevant professional groups, where you know some of your participants are members.

If your presentation was part of an event, follow up with the organisers to both get feedback on your session and (assuming the feedback was good!) to show your interest in participating in future events that are appropriate to your area of specialism.

When given positive feedback via any mechanism, ask if you can quote it in your promotional materials.

You can even ask for a LinkedIn 'recommendation' that will be permanently visible on your profile for every visitor to see.

Pro tip: Often, you can capture LinkedIn recommendations from people who have attended your presentation and want to Link-In with you.

When people have been in a presentation I've made and want to connect with me, they will often start their invite with something like, "Loved your presentation, and the insights you shared. Would you like to connect?" I seize this opportunity by replying with, "Thanks for your kind words. I'd love to connect! While my presentation is fresh in your mind, please would you leave me a LI

Recommendation? Just a few lines would really help me in getting my message out there." And I include a link they can click to leave the recommendation.

This approach has netted me a great number of recommendations on LinkedIn.
Check out my profile to see them:
https://www.linkedin.com/in/davidduffett/
Since people are people – and they love connecting with people personally, don't be shy about suggesting an in-person meet up with any individuals whom you feel resonate with you.

Make the most of the work you've already done!

As already mentioned, you may wish to share your slides and/or other resources and reference materials after your session along with making a recording available, if one was made. Repetition is the mother of learning!

People very much appreciate a 'key takeaways' document or 'cheat sheet' too.

Sharing highlights, specific insights, themes or even direct quotes from the presentation on social media, especially LinkedIn if dealing with 'business' audiences, really helps to get your message out there, beyond those that you originally delivered your session to – and tagging people is a great way to show that you are grateful for their participation or organisation of the event.

Are you the kind of person that likes documentation and records? If so, put that trait to work in noting down the outcomes of your presentation – both in your own view, and that of the Sponsor. Any numbers like attendance figures, averaged feedback scores, etc. can also be useful data when you are trying to see whether there are any trends.

It is also good practice to organise your presentation materials, references, etc. in a logical way to aid re-use for similar assignments. This is very likely to be in the cloud these days, which makes sense for access from different locations and mitigates any issues that you might suffer with your laptop or tablet.

There is an almost endless list of other things you can do with the materials you prepared – blog posts, LinkedIn posts, articles or infographics (to name a few) will all help you capitalise your efforts.

Take a Step Back

Considering your own performance is time well spent. What went so well that you would like to replicate that success in future talks? What would you like to improve next time around? Was there any immediate feedback you should note down in order to properly capture before it fades away?

This process can be aided by reviewing audio or video recordings, as from time to time you may find that things went a little differently from the way you remembered them in the heat of battle.

If there is someone in your life who genuinely wants the best for you, and who has an opinion you value, have them review any available recordings too – they may identify things you missed, or be able to reassure you that something that alarmed you is actually nothing to worry about.

In summary, the best outcome of a great presentation is a win-win-win!
A win for your audience.
A win for your sponsor.
And a win for you.
By using the 7 Power Presenting Protocols to either create a brand-new presentation, or to optimise a presentation you already have, the chances are very high – close to 100% - that you have a great presentation on your hands.

One that hits the target for your audience and sponsor in terms of outcomes and is designed to get your message across with maximum effect in terms of both the structure and method(s) of delivery to your audience.

It will be well practiced, contain just the right amount of appropriate participation and will be powerfully delivered using the best of your vocal delivery, confidence and posture.

The key now is to use the contents of the 'Post-Event' protocol to extract the absolute maximum value from it for everyone involved AND those who might want to get to know you better and work with you in the future!

Chapter Ten - RAPPORT: The Rocket Fuel for Your Presentation

Imagine your presentation as a data stream, flowing effortlessly into the minds of your audience. When rapport is strong, this connection is like a high-speed internet link - clear, reliable, and effective. Information flows freely, misunderstandings are minimised, and your audience is engaged, receptive, and even inspired. Conversely, when rapport is weak, the connection suffers. It's akin to a low-bandwidth internet connection, where buffering, delays, and frustration dominate. The flow of information stutters, engagement drops, and your message risks being lost altogether.

Rapport is more than just a pleasant connection; it's the rocket fuel that propels your presentation from merely informative to powerfully impactful. Establishing rapport means building trust, mutual understanding, and a sense of shared purpose with your audience. It's the secret ingredient that transforms your presentation into a memorable experience, ensuring your audience not only receives your message but is truly motivated and committed to act on it!

Without rapport, even the best-prepared presentation or presenter can falter. Your audience might perceive you as distant, unapproachable, or out of touch with their needs. Disengagement creeps in, and the risk of miscommunication increases. The result? Dropped signals, lost opportunities, and a presentation that fails to resonate. By focusing on creating, maintaining and building rapport, you ensure that your message is not just delivered but received and valued.

This chapter explores how the 7 Power Presenting Protocols can help you establish, maintain, and grow rapport throughout the creation and delivery of your presentation, and into the post-event timeframe too. After the opportunity to create rapport in the Purpose protocol, each subsequent protocol acts as a booster to your connection, amplifying the bandwidth of rapport and ensuring a smooth and meaningful exchange of ideas.

Purpose: Aligning Expectations and Objectives

Every successful presentation begins with a clear, shared and agreed purpose. Think of this as the initial handshake between you, your Sponsor and your audience, opening the channel for communication. If this handshake is firm and confident, the bandwidth of rapport immediately expands. However, if the purpose is unclear or misaligned, it's like attempting to stream a video with an unstable connection - misunderstandings are almost inevitable.

Purpose is about aligning the needs of both the sponsor of your presentation and your audience. For example, the sponsor might want you to communicate a new strategy, while the audience's primary concern is understanding how that strategy impacts them personally. By clarifying these objectives upfront, you ensure your presentation addresses the broader business goals while resonating on an individual level.

Setting a clear purpose also creates a shared understanding of what success looks like. Are you aiming to inform, persuade, or inspire action? When this is established, you're not just speaking to your audience - you're speaking with them. This mutual alignment enhances trust and fosters a sense of collaboration, key components of strong rapport.

Furthermore, a well-defined purpose is exactly what you need to measure the success of your presentation. Whether it's through follow-up surveys, audience feedback, or observed changes in behaviour, knowing the purpose provides benchmarks to evaluate your effectiveness. With a strong purpose, your presentation's connection remains stable, ensuring your audience stays engaged and aligned with your message.

Plan: Structuring for Maximum Engagement

A well-structured presentation is like a robust network infrastructure in that it ensures seamless data transfer, prevents bottlenecks, and maximises connection speed. Without a solid plan, your audience may feel lost, frustrated, or overwhelmed, akin to navigating a webpage that takes forever to load.

Planning begins with a clear outline of your key messages and their logical flow. Start with an engaging introduction that captures attention and sets the stage for the journey ahead. Use signposting to indicate where you're headed at each stage, it will guide your audience and maintain their focus. This creates a sense of security, as your audience knows what to expect and when to expect it.

Effective planning also accounts for the natural ebb and flow of human attention spans. Research shows that engagement tends to dip after 10 to 15 minutes. By strategically placing key points, stories, or interactive elements at these intervals, you can re-energise your audience and keep the connection strong. Remember, your audience needs PROOF! (See Protocol 2: Plan)

Visual aids, data, and anecdotes should be chosen and carefully arranged to enhance your narrative. Overloading your presentation with excessive details or irrelevant information can clog the bandwidth, causing your audience to disengage. Instead, distil your message into its most essential components, ensuring clarity and impact.

Finally, rehearse your plan to identify and address potential weak points. See the Practise protocol. Think of this as testing the network for vulnerabilities before launch. A well-rehearsed plan ensures a smooth and engaging delivery, maintaining a high level of rapport throughout.

Preferences: Tailoring Delivery for Maximum Impact

Understanding your audience's preferences is like optimising a website for different devices and browsers. When you tailor your presentation to their needs and learning styles, the connection becomes more efficient and enjoyable. Failing to do so, however, can result in mismatched expectations and a weakened rapport.

In the Preferences chapter, we considered whether people are input, action or reflection led in terms of the way they like to learn things.

Here is another angle... Some people are visual learners who respond best to charts, graphs, and images. Others are auditory learners who prefer clear explanations and compelling storytelling. Still others are kinaesthetic learners who benefit from hands-on activities or practical examples.

As noted in the Preferences chapter, if you absolutely know what kind of learners your audience are, then you can tailor the experience especially for them.
If you don't, then cater for all styles.

By incorporating a mix of these elements, you ensure that your presentation resonates with the widest possible audience. For example, a slide deck rich with visuals might engage the visual learners, while sharing an inspiring anecdote appeals to the auditory learners. Including a brief interactive exercise or demonstration captures the attention of the kinaesthetic learners.

Moreover, tailoring your delivery shows respect and consideration for your audience. It demonstrates that you've taken the time to understand their needs, fostering trust and rapport. It's the difference between presenting generic information and delivering a customised experience that feels personal and relevant.

Adjusting to preferences also involves adapting to the cultural and professional context of your audience. Engineers, for instance, might appreciate precise data and logical explanations, while a mixed audience may respond better to relatable stories and simplified concepts. By aligning your delivery with their preferences, you maximise the bandwidth of rapport, ensuring your message is received as intended.

When you account for audience preferences, you're not just speaking to their minds, you're connecting with their hearts. This depth of engagement strengthens rapport and creates a lasting impact, making your presentation truly unforgettable.

Practise: Debugging and Bandwidth Testing

Practising your presentation is the equivalent of running a diagnostic speed test on your internet connection. Just as a slow connection highlights areas in need of improvement, practising reveals weaknesses in your delivery, pacing, and content. The more you practise, the more you optimise the bandwidth of your rapport with the audience.

Start by practising in a quiet environment to refine your content and timing. Pay attention to areas where you stumble or feel unsure, these are like the laggy spots in a network connection. Identify and address these issues early to ensure a smoother performance.

Next, simulate real-world conditions. Rehearse in the venue or a similar setting, factoring in potential distractions like lighting, sound, or audience layout.

Think of this as testing your connection under peak usage conditions. Practising in this way prepares you for unforeseen variables and helps maintain rapport, even when the unexpected happens.

Incorporate feedback loops into your practise sessions. Present to colleagues, friends, or mentors and ask for honest critiques. Their insights help you fine-tune your delivery and gauge audience reactions. Additionally, record yourself to identify non-verbal cues, such as posture, gestures, or facial expressions, that might affect how your message is received.

Practice also familiarises you with your material, boosting confidence and reducing reliance on notes. A confident presenter exudes energy and authenticity, both of which strengthen the audience's connection to your message. When you've thoroughly rehearsed, you eliminate buffering (those awkward pauses or forgotten points) ensuring the bandwidth remains wide open and robust.

Participation: Enabling High-Speed Uploads

Participation transforms a presentation from a monologue into a dialogue. The more your audience engages, the faster and clearer the flow of ideas becomes. It's best to encourage questions, interactive exercises, and audience feedback throughout, where possible. This interactivity acts like a high-speed upload, ensuring mutual exchange, alignment, and deeper investment in the content.

Begin by setting a welcoming tone that invites participation. This might involve asking rhetorical questions, conducting live polls, or simply encouraging nods and reactions. These small actions (which we could call micro-commitments) create a dynamic feedback loop, strengthening rapport by showing the audience that their input matters.

Interactive elements should be seamlessly integrated into your presentation's flow. For example, after presenting a key idea, pause for a moment and invite the audience to share their perspectives or ask questions. This pause not only reinforces their engagement but also provides valuable insight into their understanding and priorities.

Participation also fosters commitment. When people actively engage, they are more likely to internalise and act upon the information presented. Involvement equals commitment, commitment equals investment, and investment equals impact. Think of it as a collaborative network where every participant contributes to the strength of the connection.

Finally, handle audience feedback gracefully. Whether it's a question, comment, or challenge, responding thoughtfully reinforces trust and rapport. Even when faced with criticism, a calm and constructive response shows professionalism and respect, further deepening the connection.

Performance: Boosting Connection Strength

The delivery of your presentation is where all the planning and preparation converges. Performance is akin to upgrading your hardware for maximum internet speed—every element of your voice, body language, and movement contributes to the clarity and impact of your message.

Your voice is a primary tool for rapport. Use variation in pitch, pace, and volume to emphasise key points and maintain interest. A monotone delivery is like a flat connection - dull and uninspiring. By contrast, dynamic vocal delivery engages and excites the audience, keeping the connection strong.

Body language amplifies this effect. Open gestures, purposeful movement, and consistent eye contact convey confidence and approachability. These non-verbal cues act like visual signals, reinforcing your spoken message and making the audience feel connected to you as a person.

Stage presence also plays a critical role. How you occupy the space (whether you stand still, move deliberately, or interact with your visuals) creates an additional layer of engagement. Avoid fidgeting or unnecessary pacing, as these can distract and weaken the connection. This is where practising to a camera can come in useful, to help you spot any unhelpful movement or patterns.

Authenticity ties all these elements together. Audiences can sense when a presenter is genuine, and this sincerity fosters trust and rapport. Be yourself, share your enthusiasm, and connect emotionally with your audience. A heartfelt presentation is like a high-bandwidth connection. It's clear, efficient, and memorable.

Your audience wants to hear YOU and from YOU. They don't want to hear a script being read or a canned performance being delivered.

Post-Event: Keeping the Connection Alive

Rapport doesn't end when the presentation does. The post-event phase is like maintaining a steady internet connection for ongoing communication. Follow-up activities ensure that the connection remains strong and that your message continues to resonate.

Start by thanking your audience and providing additional resources. This could include a summary of your key points, links to relevant articles, or a recording of your presentation. These actions show that you value their time and are committed to their success, reinforcing trust and rapport.

Encourage feedback to gauge the effectiveness of your presentation. Surveys or informal conversations provide insights into what resonated and what could be improved. This feedback loop not only helps you grow as a presenter but also demonstrates humility and a willingness to learn.
Repurpose your presentation content to reach a broader audience. Blog posts, infographics, or social media updates can amplify your message and keep it alive long after the event. By continuing to share and engage, you extend the bandwidth of rapport, reaching even those who couldn't attend in person.

Lastly, nurture relationships with key audience members and stakeholders, like your sponsor. A personalised thank-you email, or a follow-up conversation can solidify connections and open doors for future collaboration. Rapport isn't just about a single presentation; it's about building lasting relationships that continue to grow and thrive.

Rapport is the rocket fuel that boosts your presentation at multiple stages, before, during and after the event. Establish rapport, and there are no limits to how high or how far you have the potential to reach as a presenter!

And, as you can see, it is both a potent thread that runs through all 7 Power Presenting Protocols AND the 'glue' that holds them together.

Action-based Summary

Establish the PURPOSE of your presentation by talking to the SPONSOR and the AUDIENCE to agree the outcomes of your presentation with a concise OUTCOME AGREEMENT.

PLAN your presentation by creating a STRUCTURE that will make it easy for your audience to digest what you want to get across, optimised for their ATTENTION SPAN and designed to lock your material into their MEMORY.

Considering the PREFERENCES of your AUDIENCE helps you to give a massively effective presentation, by thinking about your own LEARNING STYLE and that of your AUDIENCE, and intentionally creating experiences that will help them learn best.

Make sure you PRACTISE your presentation fully, especially the BEGINNING and the ENDING as these are the PRIME TIME in terms of your audience's attention. This must be done OUT LOUD and to real people if possible.

Build maximum PARTICIPATION into your presentation so that your audience feel a real part of the session, not just people on the receiving end of your talking.

Remember that golden formula,
INVOLVEMENT=COMMITMENT

Work on your PERFORMANCE by thinking about the way you LOOK and the way you SOUND to your audience. Minimise NERVES by ensuring you complete the above protocols, especially by PRACTISING the start and the ending.

Ensure that POST-EVENT activities are a solid part of your plan, both in terms of EVALUATING THE EFFECTIVENESS of your presentation from the perspective of your audience, and by measuring the OUTCOMES with the SPONSOR.

Always keep RAPPORT in mind! You will establish and build it by going through the above protocols, but it can be further enhanced by walking in your audience's (and your Sponsor's) shoes.

The greater your RAPPORT with the audience, the more engaging your communication, the more effective your presentation...

If you implement these 7 Power Presenting Protocols that you have learnt, and work on your RAPPORT creation and building skills, your presentations are guaranteed to stand out from the sea of mediocrity that is out there!

But don't take my word for it, DO IT IN REAL LIFE!

And reap the many rewards of being a Nerd that gets heard!

Thank you for trusting me as your guide. We've reached the end of this book, but not the end of our journey together...

There are some useful resources on the 'Let the Geek Speak' YouTube Channel, and at geekspeakhq.com - where you will also find details of how to book me as a speaker or to run a Masterclass for you and your team.

David Duffett, March 2025

P.S. If you find a password is required to access any book-related resources on the geekspeakhq.com website, it's **NEOQ&A!2025**

Printed in Dunstable, United Kingdom

63190607R00102